Introduction: Music for Youth

1 New friends ▸ p. 11

a) *What do you know about the new friends? Circle the right answer. You need the letters in brackets in part b).*

Asif

Katrina

Latisha

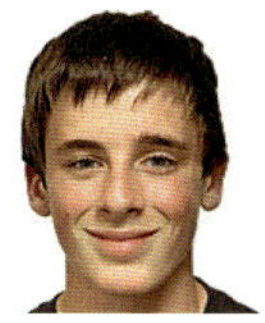

Robert

1 Katrina is from ...

Manchester. (P)	The Orkneys. (L)	London. (B)

2 Does Asif play in a band?

Yes. (J)	No. (M)	Don't know. (S)

3 The name of Asif's brother is ...

Ali. (E)	Ranjit. (H)	Hassan. (A)

4 Which instrument does Latisha play?

The steel drum. (C)	The fiddle. (U)	The keyboard. (F)

5 Is Robert in the festival?

Yes. (L)	No. (K)	Don't know. (P)

6 Robert is from ...

the USA. (R)	Australia. (T)	Canada. (E)

7 Who is a DJ back home?

Latisha. (I)	Asif. (E)	Robert. (E)

8 Does Robert play an instrument?

Yes. (R)	No. (C)	Don't know. (L)

9 Latisha is from ...

Birmingham. (E)	Manchester. (O)	London. (B)

10 Latisha loves ...

football. (W)	ice hockey. (G)	squash. (N)

11 In the evening the students go to watch ...

Katrina's fiddle band. (M)	Latisha's steel drum band. (K)	Hassan's Asian Fusion band. (B)

b) *Now write the letters next to your answers in the boxes. If your answers are correct, the letters make a message. Here are the question numbers:*

10	7	1	4	9	2	6		11	3	8	5
		L									

The message is: ______________________________!

2 Who says what? ▸ p. 11

a) Match the sentences to the speakers. Then check your answers on pp. 7–11 of your student's book.

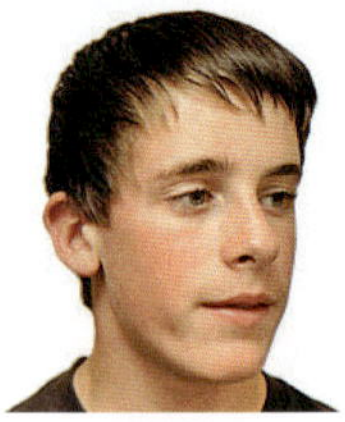

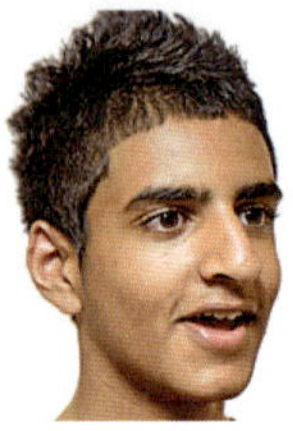

I'm just a roadie for my brother's band.

It's one of the Orkney Islands – north of Scotland.

But I DJ.

I love ice hockey.

Oh, my game's football.

The islands are beautiful, but I'd really like to see London one day.

I'll mail you some photos.

Let's keep in touch.

Tell Hassan to come and do a gig in Manchester.

b) Write three sentences each about Asif, Katrina, Latisha and Robert.

Asif lives ______

Katrina comes ______

Latisha ______

Robert ______

3 WORDS Music words ▸ p. 11

a) Find and write the music words in the list, then cross them out of the puzzle.

~~b~~	~~a~~	~~n~~	~~d~~	s	~~k~~	~~e~~	~~y~~	~~b~~
~~o~~	~~a~~	~~r~~	~~d~~	p	c	o	n	c
e	r	t	o	e	l	e	c	t
r	i	c	g	u	i	t	a	r
a	g	i	g	f	l	u	t	e
t	r	u	m	p	e	t	n	c
h	o	i	r	e	d	r	u	m
s	h	r	e	c	o	r	d	e
r	o	v	i	o	l	i	n	x

band

keyboard

______

______

______

______

______

______

______

______

b) Which letters are still in the puzzle? Put them in the correct order to make a new word for a musical instrument.

0303 The instrument is: ______________________ .

Now you

Write two paragraphs about music. How many different kinds of music do you know? What is your favourite kind of music? What kind of music don't you like? Would you like to go to a music festival? What do you think is good about music festivals? What do you think is maybe not so good? Read the picture story again on pp. 7–11 of your student's book for ideas.

____

____

____

____

____

____

____

____

0305 ______________________

Revision

1 WORDS Lists ▸ p. 11

First find the group words or phrases. Write them at the top of the lists. Then write the words in the correct lists.

throat • valley • *places in town* • fields • shoulder • policeman • in the country • forest • *library* • fireman • department store • police station • hills • stomach • parts of the body • knee • post office • teacher • jobs • hospital • waitress • lake • leg • leisure centre • engineer • village • head • shop assistant

1 *Places in town*	2	3	4
library			

0401

2 They all love music (Simple present: positive and negative sentences) ▸ p. 11

Complete with verbs in the simple present.

Robert *comes* (come) from Canada. Katrina, Latisha and Asif all *come* (come) from the UK, but they *don't know* (~~know~~) anybody in Birmingham. When they ______ (meet) at the music festival, they soon ______ (become) good friends.

The four friends all ______ (love) music. Asif ______ (like) rap and Asian Fusion. Robert, Latisha and Katrina ______ (~~know~~) anything about Asian Fusion, but Asif ______ (tell) them that it's a mixture of western and Asian music. Asif ______ (~~know~~) much about folk music, but Katrina ______ (love) it. She ______ (play) the fiddle in the school band and she ______ (practise) every day. Latisha's instrument is the steel drum, but she ______ (~~practise~~) as often as Katrina.

Robert and Asif ______ (~~play~~) an instrument, but they both ______ (know) lots about music. They all ______ (think) the festival is great.

0503

3 Do they play an instrument? (Simple present: yes/no questions and short answers) ▸ p. 11

*Hassan wants to know about Asif's new friends. Write Hassan's questions with **do** or **does** and Asif's answers.*

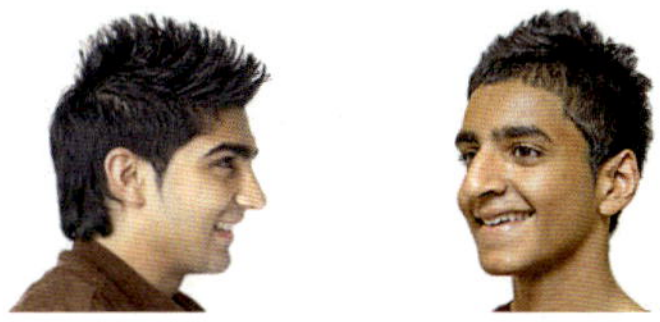

Hassan's questions: **Asif's answers:**

1 Robert – come from Canada ?

Does Robert come from Canada? – Yes, he does.

2 Robert – play in a band ?

_______________ – _______________

3 Katrina and Latisha – play an instrument ?

_______________ – _______________

4 Latisha – come from the Orkneys ?

_______________ – _______________

5 your friends – know what Asian Fusion is ?

_______________ – _______________

6 they – want to come to our gig ?

_______________ – _______________

0504 Great! Your new friends are cool!

4 Odd one out ▸ p. 11

Find the odd one out and write it down. Then write the letters to find the new word ▸.

1 cool • great • nice • awful • fantastic — awful (3) f

2 waiter • painter • cooker • presenter • writer — _______ (5) ___

3 rainy • foggy • stormy • noisily • cloudy — _______ (4) ___

4 pub • factory • town • station • cinema — _______ (1) ___

5 monkey • bear • lion • budgie • hippo — _______ (5) ___

6 river • sea • view • lake • water — _______ (1) ___

7 dishwasher • garage • cooker • sink — _______ (2) ___

8 skirt • shoulder • shirt • trousers • jacket — _______ (5) ___

0402 ▶ Latisha, Katrina, Robert and Asif meet at a _______________ in Birmingham.

5 What are they doing? (Present progressive) ► p. 11

a) Complete the sentences with the present progressive.

1

2

3

4

buy – tickets – workshop	chat – Katrina	have – snack	practise – fiddle

1 Just now the boys *are buying tickets for a workshop.*

2 Right now Latisha ______________________.

3 Now Robert and Asif ______________________.

4 Now Katrina ______________________.

b) Circle the correct form, simple present or present progressive.

1 Robert (doesn't like / isn't liking) waiting, but just now he ('s waiting / he waits) for Latisha and Katrina.

2 *Robert* Listen. Somebody (practises / is practising) the fiddle. Maybe it's Katrina.
She (practises / 's practising) every day. But Latisha (isn't practising / doesn't practise) every day. So where is she?

3 *Asif* Well, she (phones / 's phoning) her family every evening.
Maybe she (phones / 's phoning) now.
0605 Maybe she ('s telling / tells) everybody at home about our fantastic Asian Fusion band!

6 They went to Hassan's gig (Simple past: positive and negative statements) ► p. 11 • GF 1a (p. 149)

Find the correct forms to complete the text.

answered • cheered • didn't get • didn't hear • didn't see • felt • found • had • looked • made • said • waved • *went* • were

Last night Robert and his new friends *went* to Hassan's gig. There __________ lots of people there.

From the audience Asif __________ to his brother, but Hassan __________ him.

Hassan __________ really cool with his keyboard.

After the concert Hassan __________ Asif and the others. He __________, 'We __________ a few mistakes in the second song.'

'Well, we __________ any mistakes,' Katrina __________. 'So you __________ it very wrong. Everybody __________ a fantastic time.'

0606 'And it __________ great when everybody __________ at the end!' Hassan said.

7 After the festival (Simple past: questions and short answers) ► p. 11

Write questions about the music festival. Then write short answers.

1 Hassan **played** in a band. Did Katrina play in a band too? – Yes, she did.

2 Robert **stayed** with family in Birmingham. ________ the others ________ with family too? – No, ________.

3 Katrina **slept** in the girls' hostel. ________ Latisha ________ there too? – Yes, ________.

4 Latisha **played** the steel drum. ________ Katrina ________ the steel drum too? – ________

0707 5 Asif **went** to Hassan's gig. ________ Asif's friends ________ to the gig too? – ________

8 WORDS Opposites ► p. 11

Which words go together? Find and write pairs of opposites.

slow • rich • must • love • possible • strong • needn't • arrive • buy • stupid • lose • hate • impossible • poor • fast • win • dirty • leave • weak • sad • sell • clever • clean • happy

slow – fast ________ – ________
________ – ________ ________ – ________
________ – ________ ________ – ________
________ – ________ ________ – ________
________ – ________ ________ – ________
0708 ________ – ________ ________ – ________

9 They've already packed their bags (Present perfect) ► p. 11 • GF 1b (p. 149)

The music festival has finished. Write sentences about the four friends in the present perfect.

1

2

3

4
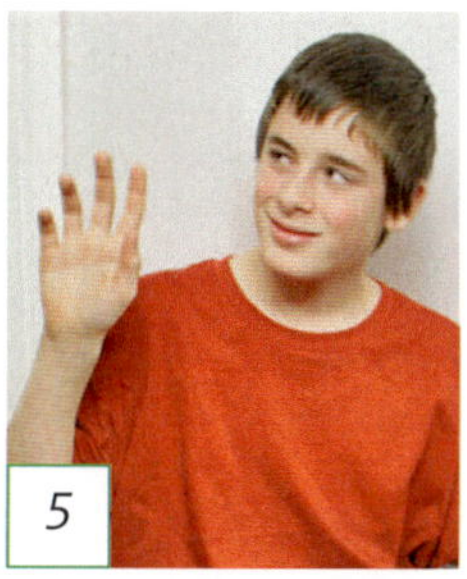
5

1 The friends have already packed their bags. (already, pack)

2 They ________ at the station. (just, arrive)

3 Katrina and Asif ________ some sandwiches to eat on the train. (buy)

4 Latisha's train to Manchester ________. (already, leave)

0709 5 Robert ________ goodbye to Katrina and Asif. (just, say)

Unit 1 My London

1 London sights

▸ pp. 12–13

Read pp. 12–13 in your student's book again. Match and write these sentences about the places 1–5 below (1 Brick Lane, 2 The London Eye, 3 Hyde Park, 4 The Tower of London, 5 Funland). Before you start, write the numbers 1–5 after the sentences.

1 It's nice and green here. 3
2 This is a great place to go on Sunday mornings. 1
3 It's on the river. ___
4 It's in the city centre. ___
5 This place is very old. ___
6 It's high, so from the top you have fantastic views of London. ___
7 This is the best place to go if you like video games. ___
8 You can buy trendy clothes and lots of cool stuff for young people. ___
9 On a clear day you can see for miles. ___
10 A long time ago kings and queens lived here. ___
11 You can relax, walk or play ball games. ___
12 You can eat really interesting food here too. ___
13 There are lots of games to choose from. ___
14 They even play open-air concerts here. ___
15 Tourists always go here. ___

1 Brick Lane

This is a great place to go on Sunday mornings.

2 The London Eye

3 Hyde Park

It's nice and green here.

4 The Tower of London

5 Funland, London Trocadero

2 WORDS All about … the London Underground

▸ p. 14

a) First, write the answers in the boxes.

1 Another word for the London Underground.

2 It's easier to find the way if you have a …

3 In the … before 9.30 the trains are very full.

4 Sometimes you have to … trains.

5 Go to the ticket … for your tickets.

6 It's cheapest if you buy a …

7 *Mrs Smith:* Which … goes to Waterloo? Is it the Jubilee?

8 *Robert:* Yes. But first we take the Central Line … to Bond Street.

9 *Mr Smith:* And then we have to find the right …

1										
2										
3										
4				n						
5			f							
6					e					
7										
8										
9			a							

0902
0903 *b) Where does Asif like to go? Write the name of the place from the letters in the green boxes.*

He likes to go to the London ______________________________.

3 LISTENING Going by Tube

▸ p. 14 2

Mark and his sister Mel are staying with their Uncle Dave in London. They're going to take the Tube and visit some sights. Where do they want to go? Write down the names of the four Tube stations.

Info box

The Tube was the world's first underground. It started in 1863! About three million people ride on the Tube every day.

1 ______________________ 2 ______________________

3 ______________________ 4 ______________________

4 Word field: Transport ▸ p. 14, p. 20/P2, p. 163

Make a mind map 'Transport' in your exercise book. You can use some of the words in the list more than once. Add other words too.

airport • bus stop • eastbound • ferry • flight • gate • lorry • plane • platform • railway • return ticket • river • road • sea • ship • single ticket • taxi • ticket office • train • station • tram • Travelcard • Tube

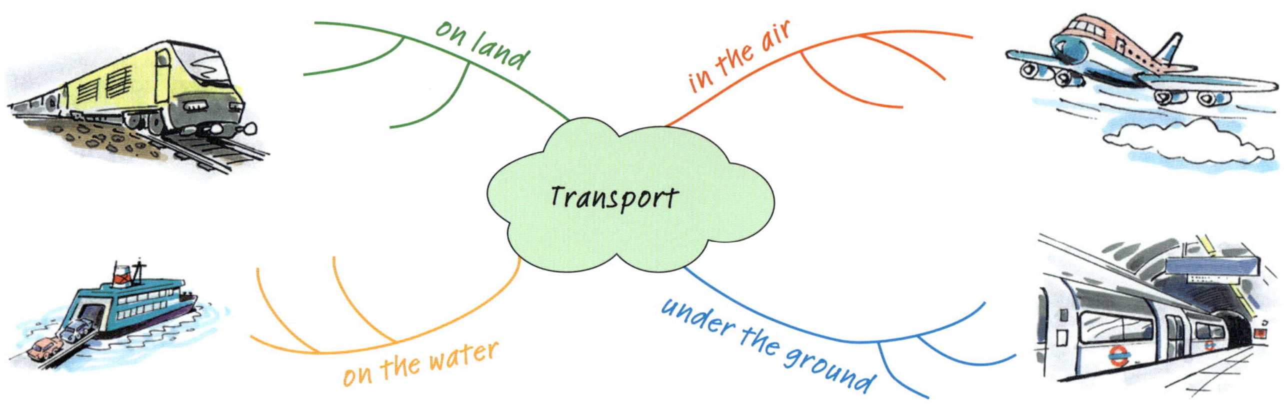

Now you

Which is the best way to travel? Say why. Write five sentences in your exercise book.
1004 *Ideas:* ***safe – dangerous, fast – slow, interesting – boring, expensive – cheap***

5 REVISION We had a great time (Simple past) ▸ p. 15 • GF 1a (p. 149)

Mel writes an e-mail to her best friend. Write the verbs in the simple past.

Hi from London!

It's fantastic here! Yesterday we *had* (have) a great day in town – and we *didn't get* (get). lost[1]. We soon ____ (find) our way on the Tube, but we ____ (walk) for miles too. We ____ (visit) two of the biggest museums. We even ____ (see) 'The Gherkin'. We ____ (go) to Buckingham Palace, but we ____ (do) the tour. So we ____ (see) the Queen – ha ha! We ____ (buy) some postcards, but we ____ (buy) any presents. Mark likes to take silly photos. Do you know where he ____ (take) this one?

Love, Mel

I think Mark took this photo at

1005 ____________________.

[1] get lost *sich verlaufen*

6 REVISION What did they do yesterday? (Simple past: questions) ▸ p. 15

*Make questions about Mel and Mark. Then write short answers. You'll find the answers in exercise **5** (p. 10).*

1 they – visit a museum ?

Did they visit a museum? – Yes, they did.

2 Mel – buy presents ?

__________ – __________

3 they – see 'The Gherkin' ?

__________ – __________

4 they – do the Buckingham Palace tour ?

__________ – __________

5 Mark – take photos ?

__________ – __________

6 they – get lost ?

__________ – __________

7 they – have a good time ?

1106

__________ – __________

7 WORDS Word building ▸ p. 15, p. 163

***a)** Which parts go together? Find and write the pairs. One word or two words?*

post	ticket	bus	rush	card	air	plat	sound
hour	form	east	machine	file	bound	stop	port

One word: postcard, __________

Two words: ticket machine, __________

***b)** Now complete with words from a).*

1 Our train to Bristol leaves from __________ 5.

2 Can we buy our tickets from a __________ over there?

3 There are lots of people at the __________. The bus will be full.

4 The Tube trains and buses are always full in the __________ before 9.30.

8 WRITING COURSE Part 1: A postcard (Writing better sentences)

► p. 15, p. 22/P6 • SF (p. 146)

a) *How can you make your sentences better? Think carefully and tick (✓) four boxes:*

- use more adjectives like *great*, *interesting* ☐
- use very short sentences ☐
- use adverbs like *very*, *really*, *a lot*, *usually* ☐
- use time phrases like *every day*, *in the mornings* ☐
- use linking words like *and*, *but*, *so*, *because* ☐
- start every sentence with *I*, *We* or *It* ☐

b) *Mark examples of adjectives, adverbs, time phrases and linking words on the postcards. Which postcard is more interesting, Ben's postcard or Sam's postcard? Why? Complete the sentence under the postcards.*

1

Dear Asif

We're in Wales. It's nice here. It has rained a bit. It's sunny too. We're in a B&B. The breakfast is good. My room is small. We went to a castle. It was nice. We're going to visit a museum too.

Love, Ben

2

Dear Asif

We're in Wales and we're having a great time. On Monday it rained so we went to a museum, but now it's warm and sunny. We're staying at a really nice B&B. My room is a bit small, but the breakfast is fantastic. The people are nice too. We usually walk on the beach in the mornings. Yesterday we visited Cardiff Castle – It's really interesting and we liked it a lot.

Love, Sam

I think ______ is more interesting than ______ because ______

______

c) *You are on holiday in London. Write a postcard to a friend. Say where you are, what the weather is like, what you did yesterday, what you are going to do tomorrow. Use the more interesting postcard in b) for ideas.*

Dear ______

______

______

______

______

______

______

______

______

Fun fact

In London there are more than 6000 restaurants, 5000 pubs, 100 theatres – and 300 different languages!

9 PRONUNCIATION [aʊ] or [əʊ]? ▸ p. 16 3

Which words are like mouse *[aʊ] and which are like* mole *[əʊ]? Listen, say, match and write two lists.*

underground		toast	

1309

10 Extra REVISION Mel and Mark (Present perfect) ▸ p. 16 • GF 1b (p. 149)

Write sentences in the present perfect with **already** *or* **not ... yet**.

1  ✔
Mel – write six postcards

2  ✘
Mark – collect information for his London project

3  ✘
They – drive in London taxi

4  ✔
Mark – spend all his pocket money

5  ✘
They – take a boat trip on the Thames

6  ✔
Mel – buy something – at Brick Lane

1 Mel has already written six postcards.

2 Mark hasn't

3

4

5

1310 6

11 Word field: Food

▸ p. 16, p. 24/P10, p. 164

What do they like to eat? Match the food words with the people. Write the words in the correct lists.

apples • bacon • bananas • beef • carrots • cherries • lamb • lemons • lettuce • mushrooms • onions • peas • potatoes • pork • sausages • strawberries • turkey

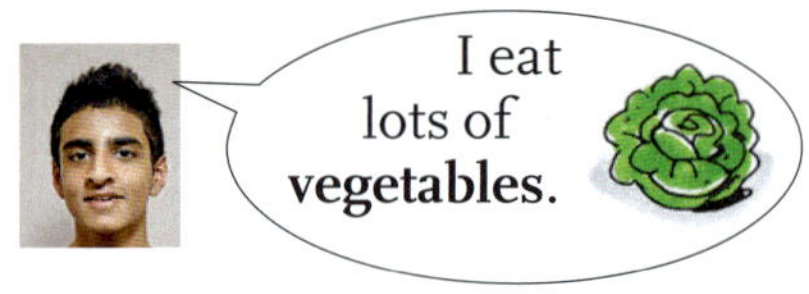

bacon, ______	apples, ______	carrots, ______
______	______	______
______	______	______

1411

12 What have they done? When did they do it? (Pres. perf./Simple past)

▸ p. 17 • GF 1 (p. 149)

Choose and write the correct form from the brackets.

1 Has Asif been on the London Eye yet? (Has Asif been/Was Asif)

Yes, he has. He ______ on the Eye yesterday with Robert and his parents. (has been/was)

2 Robert ______ Bangladeshi food too. (has tried/tried)

He ______ Bangladeshi food when he was in Brick Lane with Asif. (tried/has tried)

3 The Smiths ______ some great photos of London. (took/have taken)

They ______ them from the London Eye yesterday. (took/have taken)

4 Robert ______ a London musical too. (saw/has seen)

He ______ 'The Lion King' last night with his parents. (has seen/saw)

13 Extra Questions and answers (Present perfect/Simple past)

▸ p. 17 • GF 1 (p. 149)

Mark and Mel are getting ready to go home. Write Mark's questions and Mel's answers. Use the present perfect or the simple past.

Mark's questions		Mel's answers
1 – pack your bag Have you packed your bag?	–	(last night) Yes, I packed it last night.
2 – make sandwiches for the train ______	–	(after breakfast) Yes, ______.
3 – phone Mum and Dad ______	–	(this morning) Yes, ______.
4 – ask Uncle Dave if we can come again ______	–	(yesterday) Yes, ______.
And what did he say?	–	He said yes, in the next holidays!

1413

14 Extra He has been to ... (Present perfect/Simple past) ► p. 17 • GF 1 (p. 149)

*Look at Uncle Dave's souvenirs[1]. Say what he **has done** and when **he did** it. Use the verbs in brackets in the present perfect or simple past.*

1 He has travelled (travel) to America. He went (go) there in 2004.

2 He ______ (see) a wild tiger. He ______ (see) it in India in 2003.

3 He ______ (ride) on a camel. He ______ (do) that in Africa in 1999.

4 He ______ (eat) snake. He ______ (eat) it in Hong Kong in 1997.

5 He ______ (visit) Australia. He ______ (go) there in 2002.

1514 6 He ______ (write) a book about his trips. He ______ (write) it last year.

15 Extra Have you ever ...? (Present perfect/Simple past) ► p. 17 • GF 1 (p. 149)

Complete the dialogue with the present perfect or simple past.

1 *Robert* Have ______ (you, ever, visit) the British Museum?

2 *Asif* Oh, yes. ______ (see) lots of mummies[2] and old stuff. It's really cool.

3 *Robert* When ______ (go) there?

4 *Asif* We ______ (go) on a school trip with our teacher three years ago.

5 *Robert* London is so big. ______ (you, ever, get) lost?

6 *Asif* Oh, yes. I ______ (get) lost in the British Museum on our school trip. The teacher ______ (see) the mummies because he ______ (have to) look for me!

Just for fun

1515

[1] souvenir [ˌsuːvəˈnɪə] *Andenken* [2] mummy [ˈmʌmi] *Mumie*

16 Blue box: Buildings and places in a town ▸ p. 17, p. 162

Match the parts to make the names. Then look carefully at the photos and write the names.

Hyde	Lane
St Paul's	Park
Buckingham	Square
Brick	Bridge
Piccadilly	Palace
Trafalgar	Cathedral
Tower	Column
Nelson's	Circus

1 *Hyde Park* ____________

2 ____________

3 ____________ 4 ____________ 5 ____________

17 SPEAKING Asking for and giving information ▸ p. 17, p. 25/P14

Look at the picture. What do you think **A** *(Frau am Schalter) and* **B** *(Frau) are saying? Complete the dialogue.*

A: Hello. How can *I help you?*
B: We want to go on the Eye.
How much are the t____________, please?
A: Ad____________ or children?
B: One ____________ three ____________ under 16.
A: It's £ 15 for an adult and £ 7,50 ____________ for children.
B: Can we get a ____________ for four people?
A: No, sorry. Group tickets are only for ten people or more.
B: OK. ____________ does the ride take?
A: Half ____________.
B: And how ____________ for the next ride?
A: Not too long. Your tickets are for 12 o'clock. Here they are.
B: Thank you.
A: You're ____________.

1717

18 Extra Background File LONDON ▸ pp. 18–19

a) *Read pp. 18–19 in your student's book again. Then match the pictures to the seven steps.*

A

B

C

D

E

F

G

Step 1 [B] Step 2 [ ] Step 3 [ ] Step 4 [ ] Step 5 [ ] Step 6 [ ] Step 7 [ ]

b) *Right or wrong? Tick (✓) the correct letter from the boxes and write it down.*

		Right	Wrong
1	If you want to buy cheap things, go to Harrods.	P	L✓
2	You can find trendy clothes by young designers at some of the London markets.	E	I
3	You can buy cheap tickets for musicals at a ticket office in Trafalgar Square.	C	I
4	You can only use your Travelcards before 9.30.	B	C
5	You can use your Travelcard on the Docklands Light Railway too.	E	A
6	At the Natural History Museum you can see lots of famous old pictures.	D	S
7	There are lots of homeless people on the streets of London.	T	I
8	People in London like to eat lamb biryani for lunch, often in one of the parks.	L	E
9	You can find Nelson's Column in Trafalgar Square.	R	L

c) *If all your answers are correct, you have written the name of another famous square in London.*

The name is __ __ __ __ __ __ __ __ __ Square.

Can you pronounce it? Look at p. 162 of your student's book.

d) *Now complete the text with these words:*

culture • designer • half-price • noodle • *on a budget* • second-hand • skyscrapers

London has something for everybody, even for kids *on a budget*. You can get __________ tickets for a musical on the same day. You can buy cool __________ clothes at some of London's markets – even young __________ clothes. If you have time for a bit of __________, the best museums are free. When you have seen the famous old buildings, you can use your Travelcard to see London's fantastic __________ from the DLR. For lunch you can eat a sandwich in one of the many parks,or go to a __________ bar – delicious and cheap!

19 WORKING WITH THE TEXT Only a game ▸ pp. 26–28

a) *Read pp. 26–28 of your student's book again. Who said what? Tick (✔) the correct box.*

1	They've got over 250 video games.	☐	☐
2	But maybe it is dangerous.	☐	☐
3	We can choose a virtual world.	☐	☐
4	This is getting too realistic for me.	☐	☐
5	We came to see the fire.	☐	☐
6	Let's take the helmets off and try a different game.	☐	☐
7	This was your idea. Do something!	☐	☐
8	It's only a game.	☐	☐
9	We didn't start the fire. We haven't done anything!	☐	☐
10	What are we going to do?	☐	☐

b) *Match the parts to make true sentences.*

1	When Robert and Asif arrived at the Trocadero,	he didn't really want to play the game.
2	Robert didn't know how virtual reality games worked,	Robert could see his hand in the game.
3	When Robert read the sign 'Danger. Play at your own risk',	they had a good view of the city.
4	When Asif said 'Push the button',	so Asif explained it to him.
5	The streets of London were smelly and dirty,	they went to Funland.
6	When they were near the Tower of London,	so the boys had to walk carefully.
7	The boys felt scared	nothing happened.
8	When the boys took off their helmets,	because the game got too realistic.
9	They tried to find the plug	because they wanted to stop the game.

c) *What do you learn from the text about the Great Fire of London? When was it? Where did it start? What happened? Write three sentences.*

____

____

d) *Do you think the story so far is exciting, scary, boring, silly or realistic? Write a few sentences in your exercise book.*

1 Transport: What is it?

1 ______________ 4 ______________

2 ______________ 5 ______________

1901 3 ______________ 6 ______________

2 Have you ever ...?

Make sentences with the verb in the present perfect or simple past.

Asif ______________ (you, ever, eat) anything strange?

Robert You mean like real *English* food? Yes, I have. I ______________ (eat) fish and chips last week.

Joke! Sorry! ______________ (you, ever, try) our food?

Asif You mean hamburgers and chips? Joke! Sorry! Has Canada got a national dish[1]?

Robert Well, they eat yellow pea soup in the French part of Canada. I ______________ (eat) that lots of times.

Asif Sounds good. I love soup. When ______________ (you, have) it the last time?

1902 *Robert* We ______________ (have) it on my grandpa's birthday in Quebec[2] last December.

3 Find and write food words.

beef • cow • eggs • lamb • mushrooms • onions • peas • pork • vegetables • pig

1  ______________

2  ______________

3 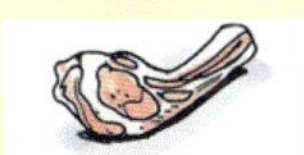 ______________

4  ______________

5  ______________

6  ______________

1903 7 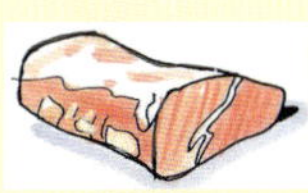 ______________

8  ______________

20 points

Now you

Imagine you were in London with your family for a weekend. Say what you did, where you went, what you saw, what you ate, what you liked best. You can use the information in your student's book. Write eight sentences or more in your exercise book. Remember to use paragraphs and topic sentences.

1904 *Last year we went to England on holiday and we were in London for a weekend. It's a fantastic city!*
1905 *First we ...*

[1] dish [dɪʃ] *Gericht (Speise)* [2] Quebec [kwɪ'bek] *Stadt in Kanada*

Unit 2 Island girl

1 About Hoy

▸ pp. 30–31

a) *Look at pp. 30–31 of your student's book again. Then read the sentences and find the right letter in the boxes. Write the letters ▸.*

	Right	Wrong
1 The Orkney Islands are in the North Sea.	K ✓	L
2 Hoy is larger than the Mainland.	I	A
3 The Old Man of Hoy is the oldest man on the island.	I	T
4 In the green fields of Hoy you can see lots of sheep and cows.	R	S
5 You can travel to Hoy by plane.	H	I
6 Lots of people on Hoy are salmon farmers.	N	A
7 Hoy has a big oil terminal.	E	A

If your answers are correct, you have written the name of somebody from Hoy.

▶ The person is K ______________________.

b) *Write these 'Orkney words' correctly.*

ldinass	phese	krsco	fslfci	mlnaos merfars	lio
islands					

c) *Choose two photos of Hoy from pp. 30–31 of your student's book (choose 1, 2, 5 or 6). Describe the photos in a paragraph each. Use* **on the right/left, in the foreground/background/middle, at the top/bottom***. Read out your description in class. The class must guess the photo.*

2 Word field: Town and country

► p. 30, p. 38/P1, p. 168

a) *Fill in the missing letters.*

Town and city words		Country words	
poli__e sta__ion	a i rpo r t	f__ __lds	co__st
tr__ __fic	sports cent__ __	qu__ __t	for__st
b__sy	cathedr__l	v__lley	h__lly
ca__ __ark	under__ro__nd	b a y	m__ __ntains
t__eatre	tr__m	fa__ __house	cli__ __s
mos__ue	d__rty	__anal	roc__s

b) *Now write the two word lists in alphabetical order.*

Town words: airport, __________

____

____

Country words: bay, __________

____

2102

3 PRONUNCIATION Stress in words with three or more syllables

► p. 30 4

a) *How do you say these words? Is the stress on the first, second or third syllable? Say the words, mark the stress and write 1, 2 or 3 in the box. Then listen to the words and check your answers.*

1 announcement	2	6 electric		11 introduction	
2 biology		7 electricity		12 opinion	
3 capital		8 engineer		13 realistic	
4 dangerous		9 excited		14 recording	
5 description		10 explorer		15 saxophone	

b) *Now think of more 'long' words (words with three or more syllables) and write them in the lists.*

1 Long words with the stress on the **first** syllable: __________

____

2 Long words with the stress on the **second** syllable: __________

____

3 Long words with the stress on the **third** syllable: __________

____

2103

4 REVISION What do you think they'll do? (will-future) ▸ p. 32 • GF 2a (p. 150)

What do you think your best friend will do next weekend? Write two sentences each, one with ***will ('ll)*** *and one with* ***won't****. You can start with* ***I think …, Maybe …, I'm sure …***

1 sleep late | get up early

I think he/she 'll sleep late. I'm sure he/she won't get up early.

2 stay at home all the time | go out with friends

____

3 watch TV or DVDs | clean his/her room

____

4 do his/her homework | stay in bed all day

2204 ____

5 I'll answer it (will for spontaneous decisions) ▸ p. 32 • GF 2b (p. 150)

Look at the pictures. What do you think Katrina will say? Use the words under the pictures and ***will ('ll)*** *or* ***won't****.*

answer

I'll answer it.

____

help

Just a minute. ____________

____

tell Mum

Don't worry, Dad! ____________

____

get some in Kirkwall

No problem. ____________

____

look for

No, I'm doing my homework.

____

meet – in ten minutes

OK. ____________

____

Just for fun

2205

6 WORDS All about ... electronic media

► p. 33

Find and write the computer and phone words.

m	o	b	i	l	e	d	m	t
e	g	m	n	o	u	o	c	e
s	c	j	t	g	c	w	l	x
s	s	e	e	o	h	n	d	t
a	s	u	r	f	a	l	w	k
g	r	i	n	g	t	o	n	e
e	l	s	e	n	d	a	s	h
g	p	v	t	v	i	d	e	o
p	e	-	m	a	i	l	h	r

2306

►	▼
mobile	message

Fun fact
In December 2006 for the first time there were more mobiles in Germany than people!

Now you

What do you think these text messages mean?

1 C u 2nite See you tonight.

2 R u ok? ______

3 U r gr8 ______

4 C u l8r ______

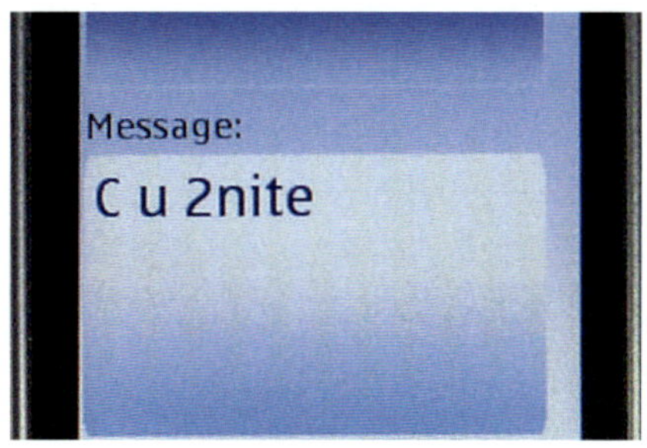

7 WORDS Word building: Verbs and nouns

► p. 33

Verb forms and noun forms are sometimes the same: (to) ***phone***, ***the phone****. Sometimes they are different: (to)* ***argue***, ***an argument****. Complete the lists.*

VERB: (to) ...	NOUN: the ...	VERB: (to) ...	NOUN: the ...
answer	answer	live	
arrive	arrival	mix	
build		rehearse	
call			smell
describe		smile	
explore			sound
	flight		start
	invitation	swim	
laugh			text

2307

8 WRITING COURSE Part 2: An e-mail to a friend (Using paragraphs)

p. 33, p. 40/P6 • SF (p. 146)

a) What is important when you write an e-mail? Tick (✓) four boxes.

- You needn't start with a greeting. ☐
- Make your opening sentence interesting. ☐
- At the beginning say what your e-mail is about. ☐
- Write a new paragraph for each new idea. Use *First, ..., After that ...* ☐
- Finish with something personal. ☐
- You needn't finish with a closing phrase. ☐

b) Now read Katrina's e-mail to Latisha and put the parts in the correct order. Write the numbers 1–4 in the boxes.

First, I'll tell you something about my island. Hoy is one of about 70 Orkney Islands – people live on 20 of them. It's the second biggest island – and the hilliest too. It's about ten miles long and about four miles across. The most famous thing is the Old Man of Hoy, a huge rock. Film-makers love it. ☐

Must stop now and do my homework. I hope you like the photos.
Write back soon and tell me what you do in exciting Manchester!
Love, Kat ☐

Now a bit about life here. Well, it's very quiet. There aren't many places to go – there's only one shop! But it's great to live close to the sea. It's healthy too. You can walk for miles. I like to watch the sea and climb over the rocks. People here are very friendly – but you can't live without a computer and a mobile! ☐

Hi Tish!
I promised to tell you something about where I live, so here's some info.
Hope you find it interesting. ☐

c) Write an e-mail to a new friend in your exercise book. Tell him/her about your town or village: where it is, what it looks like, how big it is, if there is anything famous there. Then write about life in your town or village, what you do, where you go in your free time. Give your e-mail a structure: a greeting, an interesting opening sentence, a new paragraph for each main idea and a personal ending. You can use Katrina's e-mail for ideas.

9 SPEAKING Telephone messages

▸ p. 33

You are visiting your cousin Nick in England. Suddenly the phone rings, but there's nobody at home. You take the call, then you write a message.

a) *Put in the missing words of the telephone call. Then put the sentences in the right order. Write 1–7 in the boxes.*

Oh. ______ is … (*your name*) … ______, Nick's cousin from Germany. I'm ______, but Nick ______ just now. ☐

Hello, *this* is Mike *speaking.* Can I *speak to* Nick, please? ☐

Thanks, great. I'd like that. I'll write Nick a ______. ☐

Well, can you ______ him there's a party tonight at the sports club at seven. And can you ask him to ______, please? He's got my number. You can come to the party too, if you want. ☐

Yes, of course. ☐

Oh, well, can you ______ a message, please? ☐

OK. Thanks. See you! ☐

b) *Now write the message for Nick.*

From: … ______

For: … ______

Message: ______

______

2509

10 REVISION What will happen if …? (Conditional sentences type 1)

▸ p. 34 • GF 3a (p. 151)

It's Monday morning. Katrina has to get up, but she's still tired. What will happen if she doesn't get up soon? Write sentences with **If** *… and* **will/won't**.

1 not get up soon	–	leave home too late
2 leave home too late	–	not get the ferry
3 not get the ferry	–	not get the school bus
4 not get the school bus	–	not get to school in time for lessons on Monday
5 take the next ferry at 14.05	–	not get to school until 4 pm

1 If she doesn't get up soon, *she'll leave home too late.*

2 If she leaves home too late, ______.

3 If ______, she won't get the school bus.

4 If she doesn't get the school bus, ______.

2510 5 If she takes the next ferry at 14.05, ______!

11 LISTENING If we went to Majorca, … ▸ p. 35 5

Mr and Mrs Preston and the kids, Leo and Marie, are talking about their next family holiday. Listen carefully and choose the correct answer, A, B or C.

1 Who would like a holiday on the Scottish islands? A Mr Preston. B Mrs Preston. C Marie.

2 Mr Preston would like a holiday in the country because …
A he would be able to go for long walks.
B he would be able to go swimming in the sea.
C he would be able to watch the animals and birds.

3 Leo thinks a holiday on a Scottish island would be … A exciting. B boring. C healthy.

4 Mr Preston doesn't want to go to Majorca because … (*two answers are correct*)
A it's too noisy.
B there are too many people.
C it's too hot.

5 Mr Preston wants to go to France because …
A he thinks Leo and Marie would be able to practise their French.
B he wants to speak French.
C he likes the food.

6 If the family went somewhere exciting, Leo and Marie …
A would have to speak French.
B wouldn't make new friends.
C would be able to do a great school project.

7 If they went to Scotland, …
A Marie and Leo would make lots of new friends.
B the weather would be good.
C it would be cheaper.

12 REVISION She didn't play games (Simple past: negative statements) ▸ p. 35

Last weekend Katrina didn't use her computer or mobile phone just for fun. What didn't she do? Complete the sentences.

1 She wrote an essay on her computer, but she *didn't play* (~~play~~) computer games.

2 She did her homework on the computer, but she ______________________ (~~surf~~) the internet.

3 She sent a few instant messages, but she ______________________ (~~send~~) any text messages on her mobile.

4 She listened to music, but she ______________________ (~~watch~~) videos on her computer.

5 She downloaded some information for school, but she ______________________ (~~download~~) any music.

2612 6 She took some photos with her camera, but she ______________________ (~~take~~) photos on her mobile.

13 If I lived like Robinson Crusoe, … (Conditional sentences type 2)

▸ p. 35 • GF 3b (p. 151)

a) *What do you think Leo is thinking? Look at the pictures and finish the sentences.*

1

1 **play – monkeys**

If I lived like Robinson Crusoe, I would play football with the monkeys.

2

build – boat

3

catch fish

4

sleep – treehouse

5

go swimming – dolphins[1]

2 If I lived like Robinson Crusoe, I would ______________________________.

3 If I had nothing to eat, ______________________________.

4 If I was afraid of wild animals, ______________________________.

5 If I had nothing to do, ______________________________.

b) *If Leo lived like Robinson Crusoe, what wouldn't he do? Complete the sentences with the correct forms of the verbs in brackets.*

1 If Leo lived (live) like Robinson Crusoe, he wouldn't go (go) to school.

2 If he didn't go (go) to school, he ______________ (do) homework.

3 If he ______________ (do) homework, he ______________ (learn) anything.

4 If he ______________ (learn) anything, he ______________ (get) a job.

2713 5 But he ______________ (need) a job if he ______________ (live) like Robinson Crusoe!

14 What would you do if …? (Conditional sentences type 2)

▸ p. 35 • GF 3b (p. 151)

Imagine these situations. What would you or others probably do? Complete the sentences with ideas from the box or with your own ideas.

tell my parents • tell our teacher • miss my friends • go to bed earlier • buy a bigger flat/house • feel happy • feel scared • get up and look round • go on a nice holiday

1 If I found fifty euros on the street, I'd probably tell my parents/feel happy.

2 If my mum or dad won lots of money, they ______________________________.

3 If we moved to another town, I ______________________________.

4 If there was a bully in our class, we ______________________________.

2714 5 If I heard strange noises in the night, I ______________________________.

[1] dolphin ['dɒlfɪn] *Delfin*

15 It would be fantastic if ... (Conditional sentences type 2)

▸ p. 35 • GF 3b (p. 151)

What do you think Katrina is thinking?
Use the words to complete the sentences.

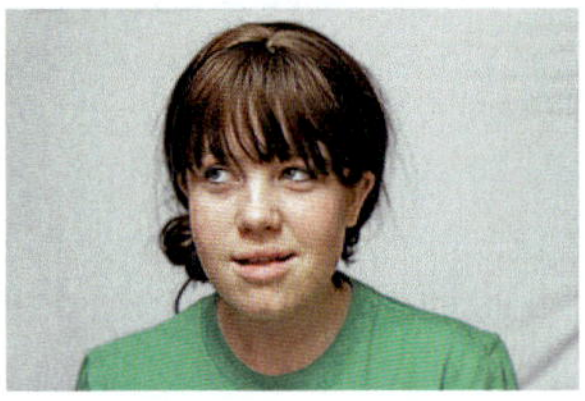

1 get – new computer – Christmas

It would be fantastic if *I got a new computer for Christmas.*

2 Latisha – come to visit me on Hoy

I would be very excited if ______________________.

3 the Beauties – always – call me Fishface

It would be awful if ______________________.

4 the Beauties – be as nice as Latisha

2815

It would be great if ______________________.

Just for fun

Boy I'm late for football practice. Dad, could you do my Maths homework for me?

Dad But son, if I did your Maths homework, it wouldn't be right.

Boy Well, a few wrong answers are OK, Dad. Just do your best.

Now you

If you lived on Hoy, how would your life be different? What would you do? What wouldn't you do? Write a paragraph in your exercise book.

If I lived on Hoy like Katrina, I would go to school by car, ferry and bus ...

16 STUDY SKILLS Using a German–English dictionary

▸ p. 35 • SF (p. 137)

You write this e-mail to Katrina. Use a German–English dictionary to find the German words. For phrases, look up the key word. If there's more than one translation, write down all the translations. Mark the correct one and write down the correct English translations.

Hi Katrina!
I hope this mail will (1 ***dich aufmuntern***).
The Beauties are (2 ***bloß***) jealous[1]. You play the fiddle in the school band – they can only play CDs! So they (3 ***machen sich über dich lustig***) because it makes them feel good. They try to look like film stars.
They have problems – not you!
Take my (4 ***Rat***), don't think about them. Tell your friends, your parents or your teacher. Nobody likes bullies. Bullies don't have true friends. But lots of people like you!

Correct:

1 *cheer you up*

2 ____________

3 ____________

4 ____________

1 ***aufmuntern***: *ermuntern encourage* [ɪn'kʌrɪdʒ]; *aufheitern cheer up*

2 ***bloß***: ______________________

3 ***lustig***: ______________________

4 ***Rat***: ______________________

[1] jealous ['dʒeləs] *neidisch, eifersüchtig*

17 Extra Background File SCOTLAND ▸ pp. 36–37

a) Choose the correct answer, A, B or C. You need the letters in brackets in b).

1 How many people live in Scotland?

A Fifty million. (G)	B Five million. (E)	C Fifteen million. (I)

2 'Clan' means …

A club. (B)	B area. (A)	C family.(E)

3 'Gaelic' is …

A a national drink. (T)	B a language. (R)	C one of the Orkney Islands. (G)

4 'Haggis' is …

A something to wear. (S)	B something to play. (L)	C something to eat. (E)

5 A 'kilt' is a kind of …

A skirt. (A)	B trousers. (D)	C shirt. (E)

6 There's a famous festival of music, theatre and dance every summer. In which city is it?

A Glasgow. (B)	B Dundee. (E)	C Edinburgh. (N)

7 The traditional musical instrument of Scotland is …

A the trumpet. (S)	B the bagpipes. (D)	C the saxophone. (A)

8 'Shortbread' is a kind of …

A cake. (G)	B bread. (D)	C biscuit. (B)

b) Now write the letters next to your answers in the boxes. If your answers are correct, the letters make the name of another city in Scotland. Here are the question numbers:

5	8	2	3	7	1	4	6
					E		

c) Write what you know about the city in b) from your student's book, p. 37. Find more interesting facts on the internet and write a paragraph.

18 WORKING WITH THE TEXT Orkney Star ▸ pp. 44–46

a) *Read pp. 44–46 in your student's book again. Who probably thought what? Match the bubbles to the people.*

What a terrible surprise! I can't believe that Fishface will be the star!

I think the film crew would enjoy our ceilidh. We could play the fiddle for them. I'll ask them.

Poor Katrina. I think the silly Beauties bully her.

1 Fiona 2 Mum 3 Katrina 4 Sheena 5 Dad

I'm not ready and I'm nervous. I hope I don't say anything stupid.

I'll have to drive carefully today. The weather's bad. We're a bit late too.

b) *When did the people in a) probably think these things? Complete the sentences with* **when …** , **just before …**

1 Fiona probably thought this *when she heard the head teacher's announcement about Katrina.*

2 Katrina's mum probably thought this ______________________.

3 Katrina probably thought this *just before* ______________________.

4 Sheena probably thought this ______________________.

5 Katrina's dad probably thought this ______________________.

c) *Complete the sentences about the story.*

1 In Assembly the head teacher ______________________.

2 The Beauties wanted to help Katrina but ______________________.

3 Sheena, the director's assistant, ______________________.

4 On Friday evening the film crew ______________________.

19 Blue box: to the doctor's ▸ p. 46, p. 163

Complete what Katrina's parents say with: to the hairdresser's | from the chemist's | to the doctor's

Dad I don't feel well today. It's my stomach. I think I'll go ______________________.

Mum I'm going to Kirkwall ______________________ today. Maybe I can get you something for your stomach ______________________. Then you can stay at home and watch TV all day.

Dad Good idea!

1 Town and country: Label the pictures.

1 c ______________

2 r ______________

3 ______________ f

4 ______________ y

5 c ______________ k

6 ______________ n

3101

2 If I had more pocket money, ...

Complete the dialogue with the correct verb forms.

Leo My friends get more pocket money than me.
If I ______________ (have) more, ...

Marie ... you ______________ (spend) more on silly things.

Leo That isn't true. If I ______________ (get) five pounds more, I ______________ (save) it for a new MP3 player.

Marie If I ______________ (want) more money, I ______________ (find) a Saturday job.

Leo No, not a good idea. If I ______________ (work) on Saturdays,
3102 I ______________ (have to) get up before lunchtime.

3 Computers and mobiles

Complete with 'electronic media' words.

Leo likes to ______________ to his friends on his computer after school. It's cheaper than phone calls.
He likes to ______________ the internet too. It's more fun than homework.
Marie likes to send ______________ messages to her friends on her mobile. She thinks it's more fun than ______________ messages on the computer. She has a cool ______________ on her mobile, a picture of her cat, Tabby. And guess what her ______________ is – Tabby too!
3103 When her phone rings on the bus, everybody looks for a cat!

20 points

Now you

If you went on holiday to Scotland, what would you like to see or do? Ideas: Orkney Islands, Old Man of Hoy, Edinburgh, Loch Ness Monster. Write two paragraphs in your exercise book. Remember to use topic sentences.

3104
3105 *Scotland must be a nice place for a holiday. If we went there, I'd like to visit the Orkney Islands ...*

Here are some exercises that will help you with your practice test 1.

1 WORDS A day in the country (Prepositions) ▸ pp. 48–49

Underline the correct preposition.

For my art teacher I had to paint a picture (of /from) a country scene. 'We can go (for/on) a walk (to/till) the old farmhouse (by/on) the river. Or we can go (by/with) bike. You can walk (up/to) the hill and paint your scene from there, Jimmy,' said Mum.

Dad listened (to/at) the weather report (in/on) the radio, and there were only a few clouds (in/on) the sky, so we went (on/by) foot.

(At/On) the top of the hill there was a good view (of/from) the area. I painted my picture. (On/At) the right I painted the farmhouse, with a horse (on/in) the yard. (Between/Round) the farmhouse and the river there were some cows (in/on) a field. There was a village (on/at) the left and hills (in/at) the background.

I was proud (of/for) my picture. Fantastic!

But then it suddenly started to rain – (on/over) my picture too. Oh, no! It looked awful.

I was afraid (of/for)what Mr Wilson, my art teacher, would say ...

(On/At) Monday afternoon (in/at) the art lesson Mr Wilson said, 'This is a very modern water colour, Jimmy. Well done!'

2 What are they doing? (Present progressive) ▸ pp. 48–49

Describe what the people in the picture are doing. Complete the sentences with the present progressive of a verb from the box.

fly • have • read • sit • swim • take

1 A little boy *is flying* __________ a kite.

2 Two girls __________ comics.

3 A man __________ photos of the birds.

4 Two boys __________ in the lake.

5 Four people __________ a picnic.

6 A girl with dark hair __________ in the sun.

3 Yesterday (Simple past)

▸ pp. 48–49 • Irregular verbs (pp. 232–233)

Write the simple past forms, then use three verbs in a short sentence. Begin with Yesterday …

Infinitive:	go	buy	lose	find	make	see
Simple past:	*went*	______	______	______	______	______

Yesterday I went to town. Yesterday ______________________________

____

____

4 Spelling (Same sound, different words)

▸ pp. 48–49

The words sound the same but the spelling is different. Complete the sentences with the correct word.

1 road, rode

He ______ his bike up the ______ to school.

2 role, roll

I've got a ______ in the school play.

For breakfast I usually have cornflakes, then a ______ or toast.

3 who's, whose

Do you know ______ book this is?

Do you know ______ coming to the party tomorrow?

4 through, threw

I ______ the ball to my friend, but it went ______ a neighbour's window.

5 WRITING Making better sentences

▸ pp. 48–49 • SF (p. 146)

The text below is boring. Write it again. Add words and phrases from the first box to make it more interesting.

after a few minutes • almost • loudly • on the lake • really • so • soon • strange • strong • suddenly • then • under the trees • very • *yesterday*

… *it was a hot day* … I went to the park lake. / I sat down … and … I was asleep. / I had a … dream. / I was in a boat …/ It was dark and … quiet. / … I found that the boat wasn't OK. / … it was … full of water. / I felt … scared. / … I heard somebody. / He shouted my name … / I felt a … hand on my arm. 'Here you are, asleep!' said Dad.

Yesterday it was a hot day, ______________________________

____

____

____

____

Jetzt kann ich ...	Sehr gut!	OK	Verbessern!
HÖREN: Ich kann ...			
... eine längere Geschichte verstehen, auch wenn mir einige Wörter nicht bekannt sind.	☐	☐	☐
... aus Listening-Übungen Details entnehmen.	☐	☐	☐
... den schottischen Akzent sowie ein paar schottische Wörter (z.B. *wee, ceilidh*) erkennen und verstehen.	☐	☐	☐
... die Wörter der Units 1 und 2 verstehen.	☐	☐	☐
SPRECHEN: Ich kann ...			
... meine Meinung im Englischunterricht frei äußern, auch wenn ich Fehler mache.	☐	☐	☐
... nach dem Weg fragen und anderen den Weg erklären.	☐	☐	☐
... über elektronische Medien sprechen.	☐	☐	☐
... die Laute [*now:* aʊ] und [*no:* əʊ] voneinander unterscheiden und richtig aussprechen.	☐	☐	☐
... Wörter mit drei und mehr Silben richtig betonen, auch wenn die Betonung im Deutschen anders ist (z.B. *'instrument, presen'tation*).	☐	☐	☐
... die Wörter der Units 1 und 2 richtig aussprechen und anwenden.	☐	☐	☐
LESEN: Ich kann ...			
... die längeren Texte und Dialoge der Units 1 und 2 lesen und verstehen.	☐	☐	☐
... die längeren Texte und Dialoge der Units 1 und 2 ohne Probleme laut lesen.	☐	☐	☐
... Texte über Themen des Alltags lesen und verstehen, auch wenn mir einige Wörter nicht bekannt sind.	☐	☐	☐
SCHREIBEN: Ich kann ...			
... kurze Texte (Postkarte, E-Mail) frei schreiben.	☐	☐	☐
... einen kurzen Sachtext über London oder die schottischen Inseln schreiben.	☐	☐	☐
... einfache Fragen zu Texten der Units 1 und 2 schriftlich beantworten.	☐	☐	☐
... meine Sätze mit *adjectives, adverbs, time phrases* und *linking words* sprachlich interessanter gestalten.	☐	☐	☐
... meine Texte sinnvoll in Absätze unterteilen, indem ich für jede neue Idee einen neuen Absatz anfange.	☐	☐	☐
LAND UND LEUTE: Ich ...			
... kenne die Namen einiger berühmter Sehenswürdigkeiten in London (z. B. *Buckingham Palace, the London Eye, the Gherkin, St Paul's Cathedral*).	☐	☐	☐
... könnte mich im Londoner *Tube*-Netz zurechtfinden. Mehrere Namen der *Tube stations* und *lines* sind mir geläufig (z.B. *Queensway, Waterloo, Bond Street, Central Line, Jubilee Line*).	☐	☐	☐
... weiß, dass in London viele verschiedene ethnische Gruppen leben.	☐	☐	☐
... habe einiges über Schottland, die schottischen Inseln und über die schottische Sprache gelernt.	☐	☐	☐

Jetzt kann ich …	Sehr gut!	OK	Verbessern!
GRAMMATIKVERSTÄNDNIS: Ich kann …			
… das Futur mit *will* für spontane Entschlüsse (bei einem Hilfsangebot oder Versprechen) richtig verwenden (z.B. *I'll help you with your bags/ I won't forget to phone you tonight*).	☐	☐	☐
… mit einem *Conditional sentence* (*type* 2) ausdrücken, was unter bestimmten Bedingungen geschehen wäre oder nicht. Dazu benutze ich im *if*-Satz das *simple past* und im Hauptsatz *would/could/might* + Infinitiv (z.B. *If I lived in London, I would have an exciting life*).	☐	☐	☐
… das *simple past* und das *present perfect* richtig anwenden: Mit dem *simple past* drücke ich aus, was ich oder andere zu einem bestimmten Zeitpunkt in der Vergangenheit gemacht haben (z.B. *Last Saturday I saw the new Keanu Reeves film*). Mit dem *present perfect* drücke ich aus, was ich oder andere irgendwann in der Vergangenheit gemacht haben (z.B. *I've seen the new Keanu Reeves film*).	☐	☐	☐
VOKABELVERSTÄNDNIS: Ich kann …			
… 'Transport'-Wörter (z.B. *Tube, ferry, line, bus stop*) richtig verwenden.	☐	☐	☐
… Wörter für Lebensmittel (z.B. *turkey, pork, mushroom*) richtig verwenden.	☐	☐	☐
… Wörter für Stadt und Land (z.B. *cathedral, coast, bay*) richtig verwenden.	☐	☐	☐
… Wörter für elektronische Medien (z.B. *download, ringtone*) richtig verwenden.	☐	☐	☐
SKILLS – LERNEN UND ARBEITEN: Ich kann …			
… in einem deutsch-englischen Wörterbuch unter mehreren Bedeutungen die passende finden.	☐	☐	☐
… Informationen sinngemäß auf Englisch oder auf Deutsch weitergeben (z.B. beim Kauf einer Fahrkarte). Im Englischen nennt man dies *mediation*.	☐	☐	☐

WAS ICH FÜR MEIN ENGLISCHLERNEN GETAN HABE: Ich habe …	häufig	manchmal	nie
… im Englischunterricht gut aufgepasst und aktiv mitgearbeitet.	☐	☐	☐
… ausprobiert, mit welchen Lern- und Arbeitstechniken ich am besten lernen und arbeiten kann.	☐	☐	☐
… die Aufgaben im Grammar File und Skills File in meinem Buch bearbeitet.	☐	☐	☐

WIE ICH MICH VERBESSERN KÖNNTE: Ich könnte …

- … Vokabel- und Grammatikkenntnisse regelmäßig auffrischen. ☐
- … ein deutsch-englisches Wörterbuch häufiger verwenden. ☐
- … ausgewählte Workbook-Übungen der Bände 1 und 2 noch einmal bearbeiten. ☐
- … meine Online-Hörtexte laut mitlesen, um meine Aussprache und Betonung zu verbessern. ☐
- … englische DVDs anschauen. ☐
- … Liedertexte aus dem Internet aufschreiben und mitsingen. ☐

Unit 3 Sport and more

1 My room ▸ *pp. 52–53*

a) *Look carefully at pp. 52–53 of your student's book again. Then read the two descriptions of the room. Which one is correct, A or B? Complete the sentence under the texts ▸.*

A

I love my room. It isn't always tidy, but it's fun. I like bright colours like yellow and blue. But my favourite colour is red – Manchester United's colour.
I've got some cool posters on my walls – a Music Festival poster, the United team, of course, and a poster of a fantastic Caribbean beach. I can dream about it on cold winter days.
My bed is in a corner and my desk is next to it. My desk is usually full of school stuff, papers and books, and my bed and chair are usually full of clothes. I've got my football and my steel drum near my bed – they're my two favourite things. Do you like my room?

B

I have my own room. It's small but I like it. I've got most of my school stuff, sports things and my steel drum in my room.
I've got some cool posters on the walls, and the timetable of training sessions for our team. We're in the semi-final! You can easily see that I play football because I've usually got my football and my football shoes next to my bed – together with my steel drum. There's lots of United stuff too. The poster is great, isn't it?
I've got a big wardrobe in my room, but my bed is often full of clothes. I'm a bit untidy. My bed and desk are old, but the blue lamp on my desk is new. Do you like my room?

▶ The correct description of the room is in ________ .

I know this because ______________________________

______________________________ .

b) *Draw a picture of your room. P. 60 of your student's book will help you.*

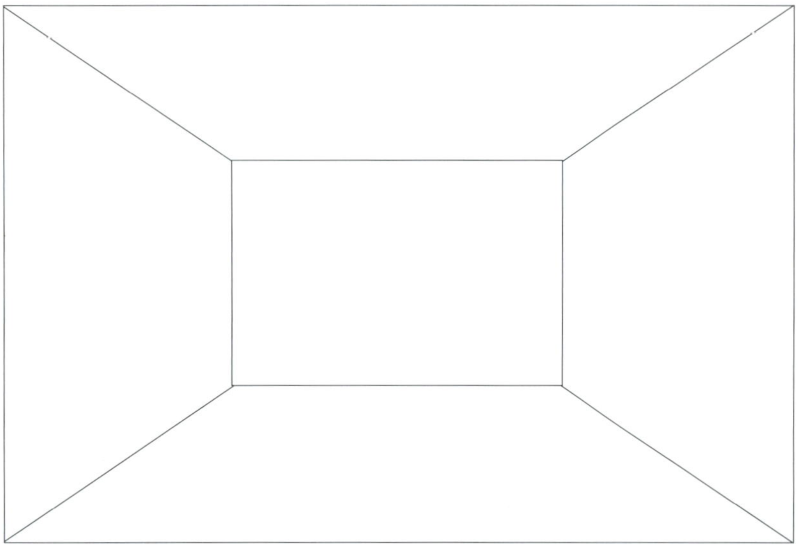

Just for fun

Boy	Dad, I don't need a new bike for Christmas any more.
Dad	Well, why not?
Boy	Because I found one behind the wardrobe in your room.

c) *Describe what you see when you open the door of your/your sister's/your brother's/your best friend's room. Say where your or their things are (on the left/right, in a corner). Describe the colours (walls, lamp, chair, desk, etc.). Which things show what you or they like to do – hobbies or sports? Write two or three paragraphs in your exercise book.*

When you open the door of my room, you see my bed in the corner on the left. On the right near the window there's my desk and chair ...

2 A profile ▸ p. 53

Write a profile of your brother/sister/best friend. Before you begin, look at the profile on p. 53 of your student's book again.

PROFILE Name: ____________________

Age: ____________________

Sex: ____________________

Location: ____________________

About him/her

Hobbies: ____________________

Sports: ____________________

Favourites

Sports team: ____________________

Sports star: ____________________

Film star: ____________________

Kind of music: ____________________

Pop group: ____________________

Pop singer: ____________________

3 WORDS All about ... sport ▸ p. 54

Write the missing words. What's the word down ▸?

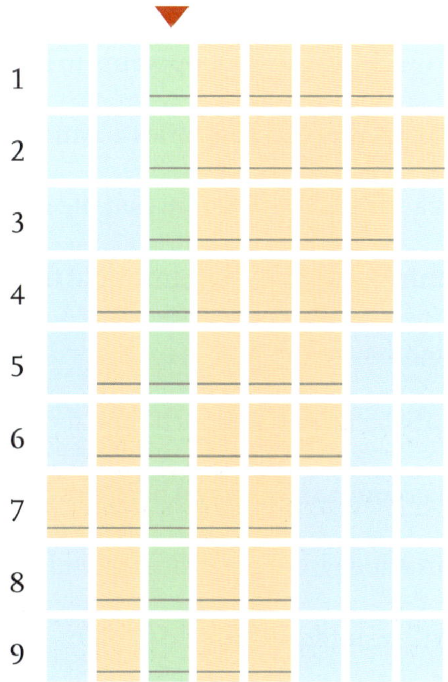

1 What's the ... ? – It's 2–0 (two nil) at the moment.

2 Latisha's favourite football team is Manchester ...

3 You play football and hockey on a ...

4 Latisha does a lot of sport. She's a ... person.

5 When Latisha scored two goals, her ... said: 'Not bad.'

6 The U14 Girls usually ... once a week.

7 The semi-final will be a very important ...

8 Latisha says it's fun to train with her ...

9 The U14 Girls' last match was a ..., 2–2 (two all).

3703

▸ The word down is another word for 'fan': ____________________ .

4 Word field: Sports ▸ p. 54, p. 60/P2, pp. 172–173

Fill in the missing letters. Then match the words and the pictures.

s a d d le   swim _ _ _ _   t _ _ _ ks   helm _ _   _ _ _ _ _et   swim _ _ _ _

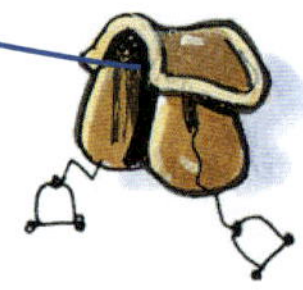

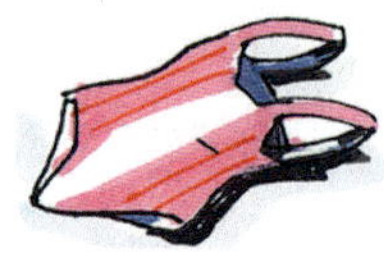

c _ _ _ t   ru _ _ ing t _ _ _ k   ski sl _ _ _   half- _ _ _ _   s _ _ _ _ _ _   ha _ _

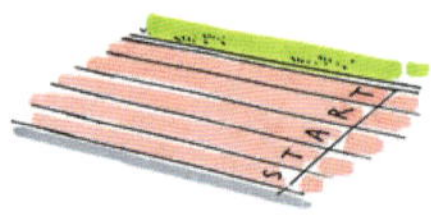

3804

Now you

Are you interested in sport? What's your favourite sport? Are you in a sports team or club? Do you watch sport on TV? Which sports don't you like? Write two paragraphs in your exercise book.

Fun fact
Elephants are the only animals that can't jump.

5 Latisha's guest (Relative clauses) ▸ p. 55 • GF 4 (p. 152)

Complete the text with **who** *for people or* **that** *for things.*

Philipp is an exchange student who is visiting the Byrds. At the moment he's enjoying the food that Latisha's mum has made. She has cooked a dish __________ her grandmother brought from Trinidad. Philipp wants to know more about the people __________ came from the Caribbean. Mrs Byrd tells him stories about her grandparents __________ left their home to come to England many years ago. She tells him that life wasn't easy for them in a strange country __________ was cold and unfriendly. She tells him about the problems __________ they had, and about the hard jobs __________ they had to do.

Latisha hasn't got much time for Philipp, but her mum says she must find time for a guest __________ has come a long way. There's some homework __________ Latisha has to do, so she hasn't got much time today, but she'll do something with Philipp on Saturday. In Manchester there are lots of places __________ will be interesting.

3805
3806

6 People and things in this book (Relative clauses) ► p. 55 • GF 4 (p. 152)

*Complete the sentences with **who** for people, **that** for things and animals, and words from the box.*

plays the fiddle in the school band • visits the Byrds in Manchester • bully Katrina • looks like a vegetable • plays for United U14 Girls • lives in Loch Ness – maybe

1 Katrina is the girl *who plays the fiddle in the school band.*

2 The Beauties are the girls ______________________.

3 'The Gherkin' is the new building in London ______________________.

4 Philipp is the boy ______________________.

5 Nessie is the monster ______________________!

3906 6 Latisha is the girl ______________________.

7 Quiz questions (Relative clauses) ► p. 55 • GF 4 (p. 152)

*Make questions with **who** or **that**. Begin with **What's the name of**...? Then write the answers.*

1 

the big wheel ... stands on the River Thames in London

Q: *What's the name of the big wheel that stands on the River Thames in London?*

A: *The London Eye.*

2 

the Scottish actor ... played James Bond

Q: ______________________

A: ______________________

3 

the famous bridge in London ... opens to let ships go through

Q: ______________________

A: ______________________

4 

the famous person ... lives in Buckingham Palace

Q: ______________________

A: ______________________

5 

the famous rock ... stands on the coast of Hoy

Q: ______________________

A: ______________________

8 At the Lowry (Relative clauses without relative pronouns)

▸ p. 56 • GF 5 (p. 153)

a) *Find five sentences in the dialogue that you can use without* **who** *or* **that**. *Write the sentences without the relative pronoun. You need the letters in brackets in part b).*

Philipp OK. Now I know that Lowry was an artist who came from Manchester (f). And an artist is somebody who paints (r). So can we see some pictures that Lowry painted now (m)?

Latisha Well, remember the deal that we made (u)?

Philipp Of course. But I like museums more than football. So let's go to the musem that the whole family and German exchange students will love (s)! I'm afraid football is something that I don't know much about, Latisha (i).

Latisha Well, football is a game that's really exciting (u).

Philipp I'm afraid David Beckham is the only English player who I know (c).

Latisha Well, now you know me too! When you leave Manchester, you'll love football! You'll see!

1 *So can we see some pictures Lowry painted now?* ____ *m*

2 ____________________ ____

3 ____________________ ____

4 ____________________ ____

5 ____________________ ____

b) *Now write down the letters in brackets after your five answers. If your answers are correct, the new word tells you what Philipp likes:*

▶ The new word is ____________.

Info box

People played a sport like football 3000 years ago in Japan, and later in Greece and Rome. In England, three kings and Queen Elizabeth I banned[1] football because it was very noisy. There were as many as 21 players on each side and players usually left the game with broken legs! From 1870 the rules[2] allowed[3] only 11 players for each team. Now football is the game that people go to watch most all over the world. After the Olympics, the Football World Cup is the sport event that people watch most on television.

4008

[1] ban [bæn] *verbieten* [2] rule [ruːl] *Regel* [3] allow [əˈlaʊ] *erlauben*

9 STUDY SKILLS Paraphrasing ▸ p. 56 • SF (p. 144)

a) *How does Latisha explain words to Philipp? Use **It's the same as** ... or **It's the opposite of** ...*

Philipp asks: **Latisha answers:**

1 What's a 'supporter'? – *It's the same as a 'fan'.* (same)

2 What does 'exciting' mean? – ______ (opposite)

3 What does 'awful' mean? – ______ (same)

4 What's a 'departure'? – ______ (opposite)

b) *The explanations are wrong. Find the mistakes and write correct sentences. Read all the sentences first.*

1 **A pitch** is a place where you can ride a horse.

A pitch is a place where you can play football or hockey.

2 **A swimsuit** is something that you need when it's cold and windy.

______

3 **A bridle path** is a place where you can play football or hockey.

______

4 **An anorak** is something that you wear when you go swimming.

4109

______

10 REVISION A training session (Present perfect/Simple past) ▸ p. 56 • GF 1 (p. 149)

Meet Nick. Nick and his friends play in their school football team. Circle the correct form in brackets.

Nick How do you think we'll play in the match next week? All our supporters will be there. We have to win.

Tony Well, Max (didn't train / hasn't trained) enough. He (hasn't trained / didn't train) last week. He (hasn't come / didn't come) to three training sessions.

Nick When (has he broken[1] / did he break) his leg?

Tony That (was / has been) about six months ago, in the match against[2] St. Wilfred's.

Luke Well, I agree that he isn't so good at the moment. And what about Andy? He (hasn't scored / didn't score) any goals in the last match. And Pete (didn' t play / hasn't played) very well in the match against Parkway last month. We (lost / have lost) 2 goals to 4, remember?

Nick Well, I (trained / have trained) really hard. I (have been / was) at all our training sessions. So I hope I'll score a few goals.

Tony Nick, that's what Max (said / has said) in the training session before he (broke / has broken) his leg!

[1] break, broke, broken [breɪk] *brechen* [2] against [ə'genst] *gegen*

11 PRONUNCIATION Different stress in English and German words ▸ p. 56 6

a) Mark the stress on the German words. Then listen and mark the stress on the English words.

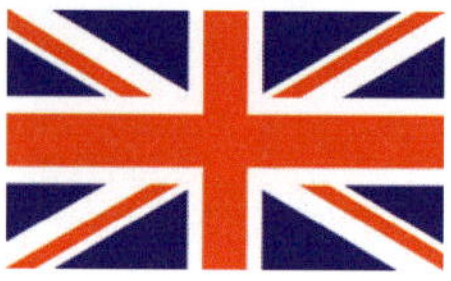   

1 accent	Akzent	6 moment	Moment
2 discussion	Diskussion	7 national	national
3 electricity	Elektrizität	8 parliament	Parlament
4 information	Information	9 realistic	realistisch
5 million	Million	10 transport	Transport

4211 *b) Find the word with the same stress in German and English. Draw a ☺ next to it.*

12 Words that go together ▸ p. 57

Choose from: do • have • keep • make • ride • take

1 You ride a bike, a horse, a camel.

2 You ______ in touch, warm, cool.

4212 3 You ______ notes, a bus, photos.

4 You ______ a call, a deal, a mess, a cake.

5 You ______ homework, tricks, a gig, sport.

6 You ______ a shower, a sore throat, a cold, breakfast.

13 A quick quiz ▸ p. 57

Read the questions and write the question words in the puzzle. Can you complete it in one minute?

1 W h o ... is going to watch the match?

2 _ _ _ _ ... does it start?

3 _ _ _ _ _ ... channel[1] is it on? BBC1?

4 _ _ _ _ _ ... are they playing? Wembley?

5 _ _ _ _ _ ... favourite team is United? Yours?

6 _ _ _ _ ... will happen if they lose? But they won't!

7 _ _ _ ... many goals do you think they'll score?

4213 8 _ _ _ ... don't we all watch the match together?

[1] channel ['tʃænl] *Kanal, Sender*

14 WRITING COURSE Part 3: A report (Collecting and organizing ideas)

▸ p. 57, p. 64/P12 • SF (p. 147)

a) What's important when you write a report on a sport event or other event? Tick (✓) the correct boxes.

- give quick information ☐
- give information about the '5 Ws'+ *How?* (*Who? What? When? Where? Why? How?*) ☐
- give details first ☐
- give important information first ☐
- say how the weather was, etc. ☐

b) A young reporter is writing a short report about Nick's school match for the local newspaper. How can you make the report better? What should stay in the report? Mark the sentences green. Which information isn't so important. Mark the sentences red.

Rosehill Park School played against St. Joseph's School in Bridgeford last Saturday. It was cold for the time of the year. There wasn't much sun and there were dark clouds. It was the schools' cup final.
The match started ten minutes late because the coach couldn't find his boots. Both teams made a good start. At half-time the score was 0–1 for St. Joseph's. It rained a bit in the break. In an exciting second half, Nick Scott scored two goals for Rosehill Park, the second goal in the eighty-ninth minute.
St. Joseph's goalkeeper had a bad cold. St. Joseph's were tired and made mistakes. One of their players argued with the goalkeeper. The final score was 2–1 for Rosehill, who were the stronger team. So the schools' cup this year went to Rosehill Park. Nick Scott's mum is going to buy him a new football.

c) Find information that answers the '5 W' questions. Make notes.

Who? *Rosehill Park against St. Joseph's*

What? ______ Where? ______ When? ______

Why? ______

How? ______

______

d) Now write the final report.

Rosehill Park School played against St. Joseph's School in Bridgeford last Saturday.

______

15 LISTENING An interview ▸ p. 57 7

Meet Nicola and her brother Calvin. They both play great tennis, but not just for fun. First, listen to the whole interview. Then listen again and underline the correct answers.

1 How old is Nicola? .... (14/15)

2 How old is Calvin? .... (15/16)

3 When did Nicola begin to play tennis? .... (when she was 8/8 years ago)

4 When did Calvin begin to play tennis? .... (when he was 8/at the same time as Nicola)

5 How often do they train? .... (every day/Monday to Saturday)

6 What do they do on Sundays? .... (they watch TV all day/they do homework)

7 Who do they train with? .... (with their father/with their coach)

8 Who already has four junior titles? .... (Nicola/Calvin)

9 Where is Calvin going to play next weekend? .... (Brighton/Bournemouth/London)

10 How many junior titles has Calvin got at the moment? .... (3/4)

11 What does Nicola want to be if she doesn't play tennis? .... (a doctor/a sports teacher)

12 What does Calvin want to be? .... (a tennis coach/an engineer)

16 WORDS Good or bad? ▸ p. 57

Find adjectives that describe people and feelings. There are 15 words down and 15 words across. Make two lists.

l	u	c	k	y	f	s	t	i	d	y	v	e	x	c	i	t	i	n	g
s	p	g	n	f	u	n	n	y	p	w	e	l	l	l	m	h	p	d	d
c	s	i	n	t	e	r	e	s	t	i	n	g	w	o	g	r	e	a	t
a	e	l	e	s	d	e	l	i	c	i	o	u	s	n	b	f	i	n	e
r	t	l	r	u	a	k	h	a	p	p	y	m	h	e	o	h	s	s	u
y	a	a	v	n	f	b	e	a	u	t	i	f	u	l	r	u	t	c	n
m	w	n	o	t	r	d	y	t	x	n	i	c	e	y	i	r	u	a	f
s	f	g	u	i	a	f	a	n	t	a	s	t	i	c	n	t	p	r	a
a	u	r	s	d	i	h	e	a	l	t	h	y	k	s	g	n	i	e	i
d	l	y	l	y	d	q	f	r	i	e	n	d	l	y	m	g	d	d	r

▶ lucky, ____________________

____

▼ scary, ____________________

____

17 REVISION They play well (Adverbs of manner) ▸ p. 57

Choose the correct word from the box. Be careful, you don't need all the words.

bad • badly • fast • good • hard •
hardly • nervous • nervously • well (2x)

1 Nicola and Calvin play tennis very _well_.

2 But tennis isn't easy. They have to work very ______.

3 Calvin says, 'You have to try to relax and not be ______ on court.'

4 Nicola says, 'If you play ______, you'll make mistakes.'

5 'You have to follow the ball and play your shots[1] ______,' says their coach.

6 'Sometimes you have a ______ day. You hit ______ and everything goes wrong.

4517 7 But stay cool. Forget your mistakes. Think about your next shot and move ______.'

18 Extra Background File MANCHESTER – a great city for sport ▸ pp. 58–59

a) *Look at pp. 58–59 of your student's book. Which sports can you see? Tick (✓) the correct answers.*

cycling	☐	football	☐	tennis	☐	cricket	☐	climbing	☐
riding	☐	jazz dance	☐	swimming	☐	badminton	☐	diving	☐

b) *Which sports go with* **play**, **do** *and* **go**? *Write the sports in a) in the lists and other sports too if you want.*

Let's play _cricket,_ ______.

Let's do _judo,_ ______.

Let's go _cycling,_ ______.

c) *Guess the sport.*

1 You can play it on a pitch or on ice. It's a team game. ______

2 The ball for this team game looks like a big egg. ______

3 You need a racket and a ball for this sport. ______

4 A very English game. Lots of people think it's boring. ______

5 It's like tennis, but you don't play with a ball. ______

d) *If you were an exchange student in Manchester, which venue would you like to visit: the Manchester United stadium, the Velodrome or the Aquatic Centre? Say why. Write a short paragraph in your exercise book.*

If I was an exchange student in Manchester, I would like to ...

[1] shot [ʃɒt] *Schlag*

19 WORKING WITH THE TEXT Who needs legs? ▸ p. 66, p. 104

a) *Read p. 66 of your student's book again. Then write questions about Nathan.*

1 Where *was Nathan born?* ______ – In a village in Wales.

2 When ______? – On 11th April 1988.

3 What does ______? – It means 'happy and brave'.

4 What did ______? – He learned to ride.

5 What ______? – He got some riding boots and a riding hat.

6 Who ______? – Some cousins and friends.

7 Where ______? – They went to the new railway line.

8 What ______? – He tried to jump onto a train.

b) *Now read page 104 of your student's book again. Scan the text and put these events in the correct order:*

- He started to play sledge hockey. ☐
- He won three gold medals at the Junior British Championships. ☐
- He played hockey for Great Britain. ☐
- Nathan played football at school. *1*
- He represented Wales at the Commonwealth Games in Melbourne. ☐
- He started to do athletics in summer. ☐
- He wants to be in the next Paralympics. ☐

c) *Find the words from the story and put them in the puzzle. What's the word down ▸?*

1 A kind of doctor is a ... 1

2 Running, jumping and throwing are part of this. 2

3 You can sit on this and ride down a slope with snow. 3

4 If you're in a wheelchair, you are ... 4

5 If you're hurt, you go to hospital in this. 5

6 Nathan ... his country in the Paralympics. 6

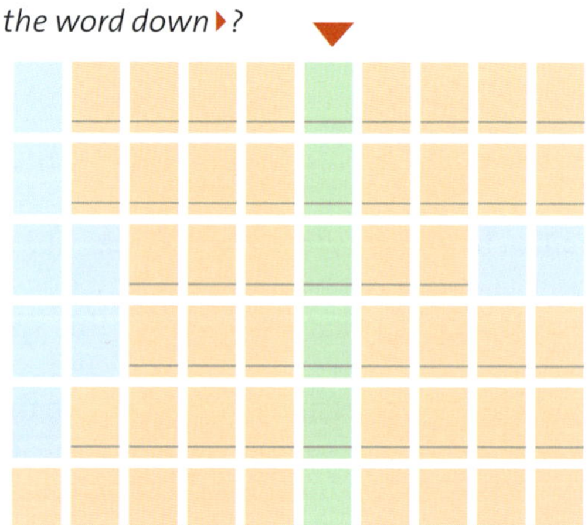

▸ Nathan has won lots of these: ______.

d) *Write a paragraph about Nathan's hopes for the future, in your exercise book. Start like this:*

Nathan is full of hope for the future because ...

1 Label the pictures.

1 g____________ *4* ____________

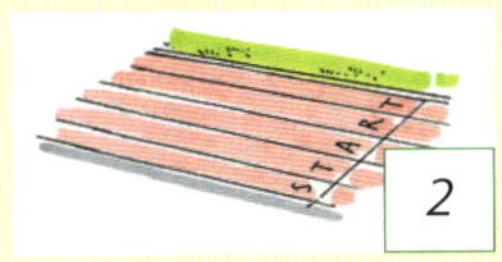

2 ____________ *5* ____________

4701 *3* ____________ *6* ____________

2 Complete with who, that or where.

1 Nick is the boy __________ scored two goals in the schools' cup final.

2 A court is a place __________ you play tennis or badminton.

3 Hockey is a game __________ you play in a team.

4702 *4* Philipp is the exchange student __________ is staying with the Byrds.

3 Paraphrasing

Explain the words in English. Use **who**, **that** *or* **where** *and choose from the box.*

stops the ball in the goal • a person or a team gets if they win the final • fans can watch football matches

1 Fußballstadion: It's a place ________________________.

2 Torwart: It's the player ________________________.

4703 *3* Pokal: It's a cup ________________________.

4 Words

Complete the text with 'sports' words.

Rosehill __________ St. Joseph's in the schools' football cup __________ in Bridgeford last Saturday.

At __________ the __________ was 0–1. Both __________ played better after the break, so

4704 Nick Scott was really happy when he __________ his second __________ in the eighty-ninth minute.

20 points

Now you

Compare your favourite sport with a sport that you don't like. Say why you like or don't like the sport. Write two paragraphs in your exercise book. Remember to use topic sentences. Ideas: **fast, exciting, interesting, slow, boring, famous players, expensive, can watch it on TV, can play it with friends**, *etc.*

4705
4706 *I like most kinds of sport, but I think ... is my favourite. / I don't like ... very much because...*

Unit 4 Growing up in Canada

1 All about Canada ▸ pp. 68–69

a) *Look at pp. 68–69 of your student's book again. Match the six captions to the six pictures. Write the letters in the boxes.*

1 A very good way to get from place to place in the snow. ☐

2 Canadian families often spend the weekend by a lake. ☐

3 If you want to be safe, you must read the signs. ☐

4 Canada's national winter sport. A

5 It isn't far to the USA. ☐

6 French is an important language in Canada too. ☐

b) *Complete the text with the words from the boxes. Write them correctly.*

1 g c p i n m a | 3 n u t h | 6 g h n a to u | 2 n g a c i n e o | 7 e o p l s r v e e s | 4 h f s i | 5 w g s n i n o e o s h

In summer people in Canada like to go (1) camping in the the national parks. They often go (2) ______ on Canada's lakes and rivers. Sometimes parents teach their kids to (3) ______ and (4) ______ . In winter when there's lots of snow, people often go (5) ______ . In their free time teenagers like to (6) ______ with friends. At weekends young teenagers love to have (7) ______ .

Info box

Canada has almost 2 million lakes and 42 national parks. Almost half of Canada is forest!

c) *Now answer the questions.*

1 Which sports and activities do lots of Canadians do?

Canadians love ______________________________ .

2 Which city isn't in Canada: Toronto, Wellington, Ottawa?

____

3 Canadian kids love sleepovers. What do kids do at a sleepover?

____

____

2 WORDS All about … adults and teenagers ▸ p. 70

a) Complete the sentences with words from the boxes.

bill	complain	grounded	hang out	old-fashioned	strict

1 Adults often complain about what kids do.

2 They think teenagers often ________________ and do nothing.

3 Jordan did a bad test, so he was ________________ for a week.

4 Sam says his parents are ________________ because they are against piercings.

5 Ashley's parents had a huge phone ________________ last month. They say it's Ashley's fault.

4902 6 Teenagers often think their parents are too ________________ .

b) Now read and match.

Parents say …

1 Please turn your music down! It's just a terrible noise!
2 You would look stupid with yellow and black hair!
3 You spend too much money on clothes.
4 Your school test results aren't good enough.
5 You talk on the phone for hours – every day!
6 If you're tired in school, you can't learn.

Teenagers say …

But all my friends colour their hair.
But I have to talk to my friends.
But rap music has to be loud.
But I just can't sleep at nine in the evening!
But I don't want to look old-fashioned.
But I do my best. The tests are hard.

c) Complete the sentences. Think carefully.

1 My mum/dad is annoying when he/she ________________ .

2 My mum/dad is too strict when he/she ________________ .

3 My mum/dad is cool when he/she ________________ .

Now you

Teenagers aren't all the same. What about you? Which things do you like to do? Which things don't you like to do? Write two paragraphs in your exercise book. Remember to use topic sentences.
Ideas: ***hang out in town**, **have sleepovers**, **play loud music**, **colour your hair**, **wear modern clothes**, **watch TV till midnight***

3 Jordan wasn't able to do the test (be able to, be allowed to)

▸ pp. 70–71, p. 170 • GF 6 (p. 154)

What are they saying? Choose the correct forms from the box to complete the speech bubbles.

1

Last week I _wasn't able to_ do the history test.
Mom was angry, so I ______________ go out.
But I've worked hard, so I ______________ do the next test.

'll be able to
~~wasn't able to~~
wasn't allowed to

2

I have enough money, so I ______________ buy Ashley a present. I ______________ stay at the party till ten.
Jordan ______________ go. He's still grounded, I think.

won't be allowed to
'll be able to
'll be allowed to

3

I ______________ go to the party because I'll be at the cabin.
It's always cool there. I ______________ go in the forest alone, but last time I ______________ go canoeing alone. It was great fun.

was allowed to
won't be able to
won't be allowed to

5003

4 At summer camp[1] (Modal substitutes)

▸ pp. 70–71, p. 170 • GF 6 (p. 154)

Underline the correct verb form.

Robert went to summer camp when he was seven. Because he was so young …

1 he (wasn't allowed to/had to) go canoeing.
2 he (had to/wasn't able to) stay with the kids in his group.
3 he (had to/wasn't allowed to) go swimming alone.
4 he (had to/wasn't able to) go to bed early.
5 he (wasn't able to/was allowed to) do activities for older kids.

Now he's 14, so next time at summer camp …

6 he (will have to/will be allowed to) go canoeing.
7 he (won't have to/won't be able to) stay with the kids in his group.
8 he (will have to/will be allowed to) go swimming alone.
9 he (won't have to/won't be able to) go to bed early.
5005 10 he (will be able to/won't have to) do activities for older kids.

5 Blue box: German 'bis' (until/till, by, to)

▸ p. 71, p. 175

Choose the correct preposition: ***until/till, by, to***

1 If there's no school the next day, Robert is allowed to stay out ______________ eleven o'clock.
2 Jessica is allowed to go to parties, but she has to be home ______________ ten o'clock.
3 Robert is allowed to stay up ______________ midnight on Saturdays.
5004 4 Ashley's party will be from seven o'clock ______ about eleven o'clock, so it will be over ______ midnight.

[1] camp [kæmp] *Zeltlager, Ferienlager*

6 He's doing a gig on Friday (Present progressive with future meaning) ▸ p. 71 • GF 7 (p. 155)

What are Robert and his friends doing next weekend? Use the present progressive and the following words:

buy presents for Ashley • *do a gig* • drive back to Toronto • drive out to the cabin • have a party • meet

1 On Friday evening *Robert is doing a gig* at the youth centre.

2 On Saturday evening ______________________________.

3 Early on Saturday morning ______________________________ with his parents.

4 On Saturday afternoon Jessica and Emily ______________________________.

5 On Sunday morning Emily ______________________________ Jessica in High Park.

5106 *6* On Sunday evening the Smiths ______________________________.

7 WORDS Puzzle ▸ p. 71

Complete the puzzle and find the word down ▸.

1. Adults often ... about teenagers' loud music.
2. *Ashley:* Last month our phone ... was huge.
3. Jordan was ... because he had a bad test result.
4. Jessica says her dad is ... He says she buys too many clothes.
5. Ashley thinks her parents are too ...
6. *Ashley:* Hey ...! Who's coming to my party on Saturday?
7. Are people allowed to ... bears in Canada?
8. It wasn't Jordan's ... that his test result was bad. The test was hard.

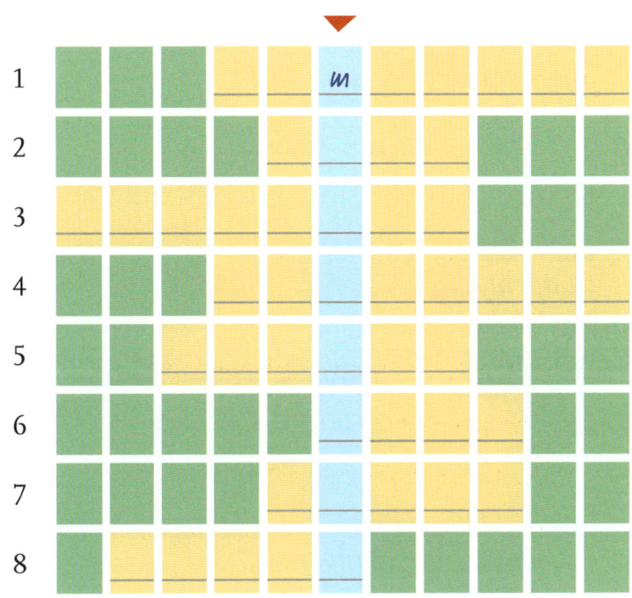

5107 ▸ Teenagers like to stay up till *m* ______________.

8 WRITING COURSE Part 4: Telling a story (The steps of writing)

▸ p. 71, p. 78/P7 • SF (pp. 146–147)

a) Look at p. 78 of your student's book again. Match the statements on the right to the three steps of writing:

Steps	Statements
1 Brainstorm ideas	Ask and answer the 5 Ws (Who, What, When, Where, Why).
2 Write	Use lots of adjectives (*hungry, beautiful*).
3 Check and revise	Check for mistakes (verb forms, word order).
	Write down all your ideas and make a list or a mind map.
	Give the story a title.
	Use time phrases (*in the afternoon, before breakfast*).
	Check the spelling.
	Use linking words (*but, so, because*).

b) Now write a story about a camping trip. Here's the beginning:

It was a hot week at the beginning of August. Jordan and his dad wanted to do a camping trip together, because they both like climbing and watching wild animals. So they went to Algonquin Park for a few days. Jordan's cousin Dave went with them.

Write the middle of the story. Use the notes below and add the words in brackets to make your sentences more interesting.

1 The first night – all tired – sleep well (*very, so*)

2 Dave – get up (*next morning, really early*)

3 Dave – walk – forest (*slowly, cool*)

4 Jordan and his dad – wait – Dave – not come back (*a long time, but*)

5 they – worried – begin – look for Dave (*after a time, very, so*)

6 They – go along path – wash room (*little*)

7 they – feel scared (*suddenly, very*)

8 be – bear – area? (*dangerous*)

1 *The first night they were all very tired, so they slept well.*

2 ______

He wanted to find the toilet and the wash room.

3 ______

4 ______

______

5 ______

______

6 ______

On the way they found Dave's wash things, his soap and shampoo on the path ...

7 ______

Where was Dave?

8 ______

c) Where was Dave? Think of an exciting or interesting explanation. Write a short ending in your exercise book and give the story a title. Then check your spelling and verb forms.

9 WORDS For or against bears? (Prepositions) ► p. 72

Complete with the prepositons in the boxes.

from • for • *of*	in • at • against
of • in • for	with • at • for

1 *Sam* The province *of* ______ Ontario stopped the bear hunt in 1999. But we have to protect ourselves ______ bears. I'm ______ the bear hunt.

2 *Jessica* You are? Sam, I'm surprised ______ you. I thought you were ______ the hunt. I'm very interested ______ the bear problem, and I agree.

3 *Sam* Some bears aren't afraid ______ people any more. In a town in the north there are even bears ______ the streets. They look ______ food everywhere.

4 *Robert* But people sometimes do stupid things and they have to blame themselves ______ the bear attacks. Maybe you guys will laugh ______ me, but I don't agree ______ you. The poor bears only want to protect themselves.

5309

Info box

Black bears can live 21 to 33 years. They can run as fast as horses and can smell maybe 100 times better than people.

10 The Feely family (Reflexive pronouns) ► p. 72, p. 176 • GF 8 (pp. 155–156)

Mr and Mrs Feely have gone on a short holiday, so the Feely kids and Grandpa Feely have to look after themselves. Complete the sentences with:

myself • yourself • herself • itself • *ourselves* • yourselves • themselves

Tommy This week we have to cook for *ourselves*, Grandpa.

Grandpa But I can't cook for ______. You'll have to cook for me.

Tommy Grandpa, you can make ______ some sandwiches. I'm going out now. When Mum and Dad left, they said 'Enjoy ______.' Remember?

Grandpa Well, what about Mo and Jo?

Tommy Don't worry about them, Grandpa. They can look after ______. They're at a sleepover.

Grandpa Oh. Well, can Julie cook for me?

Tommy Julie is in her room. She's teaching ______ to play the violin. Can't you hear her?

Grandpa Oh, I thought that noise was the cat! Hmmm. And what about food?

Tommy Don't worry about the cat, Grandpa. The cat can feed ______.

Grandpa Yes, I know that, but the cat can't feed me!

11 Noises in the night (Reflexive pronouns) ▸ p. 72, p. 177

Tom tells a scary story. Where do you need a reflexive pronoun?

I once stayed at a cabin by a lake with my dad. Before we left home, Mom said 'Look after __yourselves__ and Tom, can you remember __–__ how to protect ________ if you see a bear? Take your knife[1] with you.' I don't like knives because I once cut ________ badly, but I put it in my pocket.

It's always very quiet in the forest, but that night it was windy. Around midnight I heard something outside. It was probably just the wind, but I felt ________ scared. I imagined ________ there was a bear at the door. When I'm scared, Dad always says 'Relax ________, son. Don't worry ________ about things that are only in your head.' But I wondered ________ what the noise was, so I got dressed ________ quickly. Something moved ________ near the door. I looked through the window but it was too dark. Maybe 'it' was hiding ________ in the trees now. I didn't want Dad to get up, so I said to ________, 'Be a man! Take your knife and open the door!' But you can't teach ________ to be a man. So what did I do? I went back to bed, closed my eyes and put my hands over my ears ...

5411 The next morning Dad said, 'Morning, son! I couldn't sleep last night, so I got up, went outside and walked around the cabin for a time. I hope you didn't hear me ...'

12 They understand each other (each other/themselves) ▸ p. 73 • GF 9 (p. 156)

*Look at the pictures. Complete the sentences with **each other** or **themselves**.*

1

They understand __each other__.

2

They've hurt ________.

3

They know ________.

4

5412 They don't like ________.

5

They're teaching ________ to cook.

6

They're enjoying ________.

Now you

How long have you and your best friend known each other? Why do you like each other? How do you help each other? Write a few sentences in your exercise book.

[1] knife [naɪf] *Messer*

13 REVISION Robert's chat with Asif (Present perfect/Simple past) ▸ p. 73 • GF 1 (p. 149)

Fill in the correct verb forms: present perfect or simple past

Asif Hi Robert! I need your help! I have just done ________ (just, do) a school project about Canada's animals. Now I need some cool photos of bears. I hope that you ________ (take) some. ________ (you, ever, see) a wild bear?

Robert Only in the zoo. I ________ (meet) a wild one yet – lucky for me. But my dad ________ (see) a wild bear. Last year on a walking trip in the mountains he suddenly ________ (see) this huge bear, not 30 metres away!

Asif And ________ (your dad, take) a photo?

Robert Is that a joke? He ________ (feel) so scared that he couldn't move at first. But luckily for Dad the bear ________ (be) very interested in him.

Asif Yes, he was really lucky. Maybe the bear ________ (have) stomach problems on that day!

14 LISTENING The CN Tower ▸ p. 73 🎧 8

Robert's cousin Emma from Vancouver is staying in Toronto. The Smiths are going to take her up the CN Tower. Robert and his dad are telling her about it. Before you start, read the statements. Then listen carefully and tick (✓) the correct box.

	Right	Wrong	Don't know
1 CN means 'Canadian National'.	☐	☐	☐
2 More than 2 million tourists visit the Tower every year.	☐	☐	☐
3 The Tower is 535 metres high.	☐	☐	☐
4 There are ten fast elevators.	☐	☐	☐
5 The elevators don't go if it's raining.	☐	☐	☐
6 The Tower is only ten years old.	☐	☐	☐
7 There are 1,176 stairs to the top.	☐	☐	☐
8 People can climb the stairs twice a year to collect money for charity.	☐	☐	☐
9 Two men once carried[1] a dishwasher and a fridge to the top.	☐	☐	☐
10 There's the famous Glass Floor, 342 metres up.	☐	☐	☐
11 It can hold 25 large hippos!	☐	☐	☐

[1] carry ['kæri] *tragen*

15 MEDIATION In a national park

▸ p. 73 • SF (p. 143)

You are in a national park with your family. You meet some Canadian tourists and your parents would like to ask them some questions. Your dad says to you:

Frag sie,
- ob wir hier in der Nähe unser **Zelt** aufschlagen dürfen.
- was wir mit unserem **Abfall** machen sollen.
- ob man die **Erdhörnchen** füttern darf.
- ob man **Angelruten** ausleihen kann.

*Explain these words in English: **Zelt, Abfall, Erdhörnchen, Angelrute**.*

You:
- Hello. We're tourists from Germany and my parents would like to know if we can put up (1) ... here.
- And what should we do with (2) ... ?
- And are we allowed to feed the (3) ...?
- Can we get (4) ... somewhere, just for today?

1 Zelt: *It's a thing that* ______

2 Abfall: ______

3 Erdhörnchen: ______

5611 4 Angelrute: ______

16 WORDS Opposites

▸ p. 73

a) *Find and write pairs of opposites.*

arrival • begin • male • agree • single • old-fashioned • disagree • spicy • easy-going • stop • mild • national • female • strict • *departure* • international • return • modern

arrival – *departure* ______ – ______ ______ – ______

______ – ______ ______ – ______ ______ – ______

______ – ______ ______ – ______ ______ – ______

b) *Now choose five pairs of opposites and use both words in one sentence.*

1 *We're taking the bus from Toronto to Niagara Falls: departure 8.15, arrival 9.35.*

2 ______

3 ______

4 ______

5 ______

6 ______

17 Extra Background File CANADA ▸ pp. 74–75

a) *What do you know about Canada? Circle the correct answer, A, B or C. If you aren't sure, look at pp. 74–75 of your student's book again.*

1 The first people from Europe in Canada were …

A the Romans. (H)	B the Vikings. (O)	C the French. (F)

2 Canada's third biggest city is …

A Ottawa. (O)	B Toronto. (P)	C Montréal. (A)

3 Canada has an Aboriginal population of about …

A 4.4 %. (R)	B 4.5 %. (C)	C 5.4 %. (T)

4 Who took Canada from the French in 1763?

A The Germans. (K)	B The British. (E)	C The Americans. (B)

5 'Nunavut' means …

A happy land. (E)	B new land. (P)	C our land. (S)

6 Where's Toronto?

A In Québec. (Y)	B In British Columbia. (E)	C In Ontario. (C)

7 Nunavut is as big as …

A Western Europe. (S)	B Eastern Europe. (Y)	C Great Britain. (E)

8 Canada's national winter sport is …

A skiing. (I)	B snowshoeing. (E)	C ice hockey. (L)

b) *Now write the letters in brackets next to your answers in the boxes. If your answers are correct, the letters make the name of another Canadian sport. Here are the question numbers:*

8	2	6	3	1	5	7	4
				O			

c) *What have you learned from the information on pp. 74–75? Tell a friend two interesting facts about each of these topics: 1 First Nations people 2 Immigration to Canada 3 National sports*

1 ______________________________

____

2 ______________________________

____

3 ______________________________

____

18 WORKING WITH THE TEXT Two bear attacks ▸ p. 81

a) Read the articles on p. 81 of your student's book again. Look for these words in the articles and write them correctly.

t v m c i i	victim	p a c s e e	______	r w n a	______
f n e i k	______	o o s d w	______	t t k a c a	______

b) Where can you find this information, in article 1 or in article 2? Write 1 or 2 after each sentence.

1 A bear attacked a man and his dog. 1
2 A man and woman were camping near a lake. ☐
3 The attack happened in July. ☐
4 The man was canoeing on a lake. ☐
5 The attack happened in September. ☐
6 The man was 55 years old. ☐
7 The woman was a doctor. ☐
8 The dog fought with the bear. ☐
9 The woman was 31 years old. ☐
10 The man couldn't save his wife. ☐
11 The dog protected the man. ☐
12 The bear escaped into the forest. ☐

c) Now write the sentences from b) under article 1 or article 2.

Article 1	Article 2
A bear attacked a man and his dog.	

1 Name the activities.

5901 *1* ______ *2* ______ *3* ______ *4* ______ *5* ______

2 Complete with: will be allowed to | will have to | won't be able to

1 Robert is ill. He ______ go to school tomorrow.

2 He ______ stay in bed.

5902 *3* But maybe he ______ watch TV.

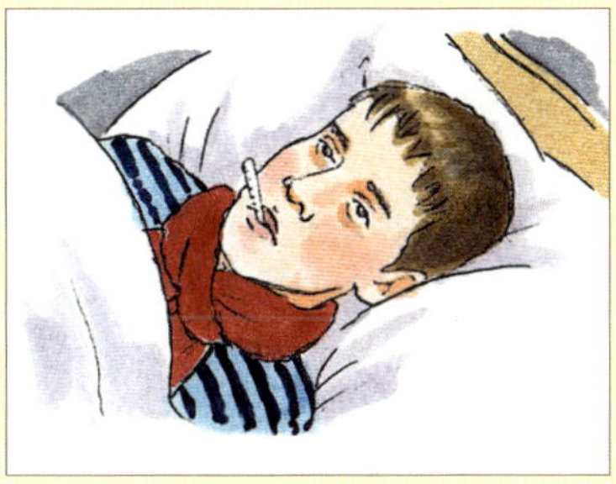

3 Complete with **until/till**, **to** or **by**.

1 In the week Robert is allowed to stay up ______ ten o'clock.

2 When he goes out at the weekend, he usually has to be home ______ eleven o'clock.

5903 *3* His gigs at the youth centre are usually from nine o'clock ______ midnight.

4 Underline the correct part in the bracket.

1 Robert and his friends always enjoy (each other/themselves) at parties.

2 At Ashley's party Jordan cut (him/himself/ –) on a broken glass.

3 Jordan and Jessica took funny photos of (each other/ourselves).

5904 *4* The party was fun and Ashley felt (– /herself) really happy.

5 Complete the words.

Jessica thinks her mom is quite e______ but she says her dad is sometimes a______. Jordan's parents can be s______ too. He did badly in a test, so he was
5905 g______. Robert's mom always c______ about his loud music.

20 points

Now you

5906
5907 *What have you learned about Canada and the Canadian people? Write three or more paragraphs in your exercise book. Structure your text and use topic sentences.*

Here are some exercises that will help you with your practice test 2.

1 STUDY SKILLS Understanding new words
▸ pp. 84–85 • SF (p. 134)

Guess what these new words mean in German. Then check your answers in an English-German dictionary.

1 art gallery – ____________ *4* safety – ____________

2 childhood – ____________ *5* surprising – ____________

3 dance floor – ____________ *6* survivor – ____________

2 Spelling (German and English words)
▸ pp. 84–85

Write the English word.

1 Titel – *title* *6* Adresse – ____________

2 Kalender – ____________ *7* Diskussion – ____________

3 Tipp – ____________ *8* Telefon – ____________

4 Theater – ____________ *9* Programm – ____________

5 Temperatur – ____________ *10* Kathedrale – ____________

3 WRITING The 5 Ws and How
▸ pp. 84–85 • SF (p. 147)

a) *Read a part of Robert's e-mail to Asif. First, mark the sentence parts that give answers to the '5 Ws': who, what, when, where, why and how?*

> I must tell you about our last big trip. We went to Vancouver on the west coast. It's a long way from Toronto, so we can't go there often. I've only been there twice. The last time was in August, in the school holidays. It's too far to drive there, so we – my parents, me and my grandma from Toronto – went by plane. Grandma was more excited than I was!
> We went to visit family – and to enjoy the city, of course. My Uncle Joe, Aunt Stacey and two cousins live near Vancouver. We saw all the city sights – Stanley Park and the Aquarium …

b) *Now write down the information in the e-mail that answers the questions:*

What? *our last big trip*

When? ____________

Where? ____________

Who? ____________

Why? ____________

How? ____________

4 Robert and his friends (Word order) ► pp. 84–85

Complete the sentences with the words in brackets in the right order.

1 Robert often DJs (on Friday evenings/at the youth centre)

Robert often DJs at the youth centre on Friday evenings.

2 Jessica went to a shop (for Ashley/a present/to get)

____

3 When Robert plays loud music, (complains/his mom)

____

4 Sam thinks that (needs/the bear hunt/Ontario)

____

5 Robert and his parents often drive (for the weekend/to their cabin)

____

6 Robert and his dad were really scared because (followed/a bear/them)

____

5 Latisha and Philipp (Present perfect/Simple past) ► pp. 84–85 • GF 1 (p. 149)

a) *Underline the correct verb form.*

1 Latisha (has played/played) for Manchester United U14s for two years. Their last match (was/has been) a draw.

2 Mrs Byrd said to Latisha, 'Latisha, we have a guest who (has come/came) a long way.'

3 Philipp (didn't stay/hasn't stayed) with an English family before. This is his first time.

4 Philipp knows that Latisha plays football, but he (hasn't seen/didn't see) her on the pitch yet.

5 On Philipp's first evening with the Byrds, Latisha's mum (made/has made) stewed chicken.

b) *Now report what Latisha and Philipp did on Saturday. Use the simple past.*

1 Latisha didn't have (~~have~~) time for Philipp on the first evening, but on Saturday morning she went (go) with him to the Lowry.

2 Latisha ________ (explain) to Philipp, 'Lowry ________ (be) an artist.

He ________ (paint) pictures. He ________ (~~work~~) in a circus.'

3 In the afternoon, Philipp ________ (~~want~~) to watch football, but he ________ (go) to Latisha's match.

4 When Latisha ________ (score) the final goal, Philipp ________ (be) very excited.

5 On the next day Latisha ________ (see) her name in the newspaper and her mum ________ (feel) very proud.

Jetzt kann ich ...	Sehr gut!	OK	Verbessern!
HÖREN: Ich kann ...			
... längere Texte und Geschichten verstehen, auch wenn ich einige Wörter nicht kenne.	☐	☐	☐
... aus Listening-Übungen Details (z.B. Zahlen) entnehmen.	☐	☐	☐
... den Akzent britischer und kanadischer Sprecher/innen heraushören.	☐	☐	☐
... die Wörter der Units 3 und 4 verstehen.	☐	☐	☐
SPRECHEN: Ich kann ...			
... mein Zimmer beschreiben.	☐	☐	☐
... meine Meinung zu Themen wie z.B. Musik, Probleme zwischen Jugendlichen und Eltern frei äußern, auch wenn ich Fehler mache.	☐	☐	☐
... über Sportarten und Sportereignisse berichten.	☐	☐	☐
... mich bei Tisch freundlich und interessiert auf Englisch unterhalten.	☐	☐	☐
... Wörter, die im Englischen und im Deutschen ähnlich sind, richtig betonen (z.B. *'programme, 'appetite*).	☐	☐	☐
... die Wörter der Units 3 und 4 richtig aussprechen und anwenden.	☐	☐	☐
LESEN: Ich kann ...			
... einen Bericht über ein Sportereignis lesen und verstehen.	☐	☐	☐
... die längeren Texte und Dialoge der Units 3 und 4 lesen und verstehen.	☐	☐	☐
... die längeren Texte und Dialoge der Units 3 und 4 ohne Probleme laut lesen.	☐	☐	☐
SCHREIBEN: Ich kann ...			
... ein *profile* über einen Freund/eine Freundin schreiben.	☐	☐	☐
... einen kurzen Bericht über ein Sportereignis schreiben. Dabei beginne ich mit wichtigen Informationen und decke die 5 Ws ab.	☐	☐	☐
... Fragen zu Texten der Units 3 und 4 schriftlich beantworten.	☐	☐	☐
... mithilfe von sprachlichen Mitteln eine Geschichte zu Ende schreiben.	☐	☐	☐
... die Wörter der Units 3 und 4 richtig schreiben.	☐	☐	☐
LAND UND LEUTE: Ich ...			
... weiß, dass Manchester eine wichtige Stadt für Sport und die Heimatstadt von Manchester United ist.	☐	☐	☐
... kenne die Namen einiger Sehenswürdigkeiten in Manchester (z.B. *Old Trafford, The Lowry*).	☐	☐	☐
... habe einiges über den kanadischen Lebensstil gelernt (z.B. beliebte Sportarten, das Freizeitverhalten kanadischer Jugendlicher, Ansichten über die Bärenjagd).	☐	☐	☐

Jetzt kann ich …	Sehr gut!	OK	Verbessern!
GRAMMATIKVERSTÄNDNIS: Ich kann …			
… *relative pronouns* für Personen (*who*) und Dinge (*that*) richtig verwenden sowie *contact clauses* bilden (z.B. *That's the boy I met at the party*).	☐	☐	☐
… mit dem *present progressive* über feste Pläne und Verabredungen in der Zukunft sprechen (z.B. *On Friday after school I'm meeting some friends in town*).	☐	☐	☐
… *reflexive pronouns* (*myself, yourself usw.*) richtig einsetzen (z.B. *The boy has hurt himself/ We enjoyed ourselves at the party*).	☐	☐	☐
… *each other* richtig verwenden (z.B. *We help each other with homework*).	☐	☐	☐
… Verben, die im Englischen im Gegensatz zum Deutschen nicht reflexiv sind, erkennen und ohne Reflexivpronomen richtig verwenden (z.B. *Sit down and relax*).	☐	☐	☐
… die *modal substitutes have to, be allowed to* und *be able to* in der Vergangenheit und in der Zukunft richtig bilden und verwenden (z.B. *Yesterday I had to/was able to/was allowed to go out/ Tomorrow I'll have to/be able to/be allowed to go out*).	☐	☐	☐
VOKABELVERSTÄNDNIS: Ich kann …			
… Wörter für Sportarten, -plätze und -ausrüstung (z.B. *stadium, court, racket*) richtig verwenden.	☐	☐	☐
… mehrere Wörter, die als Verb und Nomen dieselbe Form haben (z.B. *drive* = (Auto) fahren, (Auto-)Fahrt), richtig verwenden.	☐	☐	☐
… gebräuchliche Wörter und Wendungen für Diskussionen (z.B. *make a point, agree/disagree*) richtig verwenden.	☐	☐	☐
… Wörter für die Freizeitaktivitäten von Jugendlichen (z.B. *sleepover, go camping, hang out*) richtig verwenden.	☐	☐	☐
SKILLS – LERNEN UND ARBEITEN: Ich kann …			
… mit *brainstorming*-Techniken (*mind map, list, 5 Ws*) Ideen zu einem bestimmten Thema sammeln und ordnen.	☐	☐	☐
… Wörter erklären, indem ich sie umschreibe. Dabei benutze ich z.B. einen Relativsatz oder die Wendungen '*It's the same as …, It's the opposite of …*' Im Englischen nennt man dies *paraphrasing*.	☐	☐	☐

WAS ICH FÜR MEIN ENGLISCHLERNEN GETAN HABE: Ich habe …	häufig	manchmal	nie
… die Angaben im Grammar File aufmerksam gelesen.	☐	☐	☐
… die Lern- und Arbeitstechniken im Skills File im Unterricht und bei den Hausaufgaben angewendet.	☐	☐	☐
… bereits gelernte Wörter und Grammatik häufig aufgefrischt.	☐	☐	☐

WIE ICH MICH VERBESSERN KÖNNTE: Ich könnte …

… im Unterricht aktiver mitarbeiten. ☐

… ein zweisprachiges Wörterbuch häufiger verwenden. ☐

… englische Internet-Seiten zu Unterrichtsthemen gezielt recherchieren. ☐

… mir meine Online-Hörtexte häufiger anhören. ☐

… ein englisches *teen magazine* kaufen. ☐

… eine/n englische/n *e-pal* suchen. ☐

Unit 5 A teen magazine

1 My teen magazine ▸ pp. 88–89

a) Look at pp. 88–89 of your student's book again. Teen magazines usually have articles on sports, music, movies and fashion. Add more things that you often find there:

In teen magazines you often find articles about ____________________

____

____

b) If somebody asked you to write an article for a teen magazine, would you write about sports, music, movies or fashion? Say why.

____

____

____

____

____

____

Info box

The first teen age magazine came on the US market in 1944. Its name was *Seventeen* and it's still successful today.

c) What do you need for a video chat with friends? Look at the photos. Write the words correctly.

mweacb	rmooint	imenrchpoo	seehnodahp
______	______	______	______

2 WORDS Through the alphabet with music ▸ p. 89

Complete the 'music words'.

A	• Asi*an* Fu*sion*	J	• j___z
B	• b___p___s • b___d	K	• k___oa___
C	• ch___ • con___ • cho___s	L	• l___cs
D	• dr___ • D___	M	• m___i___l • mus___n
E	• ele___c gu___	O	• op___a
F	• f___d___ • f___te	P	• p___no • po___
G	• g___	R	• r___p • rec___r
H	• h___ph___	S	• s___ph___ • st___ dr___
I	• (musical) i___str___	T	• tr___t

6402

3 STUDY SKILLS Skimming ▸ p. 90 • SF (p. 141)

a) Skim the text and answer the questions below.

And the winner is …

About the show
It has different names in different countries, but it's the same all over the world. It's a show that TV audiences love. If you think you can sing, if you want to become famous and maybe rich, if you want to meet famous people and be everybody's favourite, then here's the show where you can try your luck.
Three or four famous people listen and say what they think. If you're good, you come back again next time. If not, that's the end. You must leave the show – and a career as a pop star will always be just a dream …

What's 'The X Factor'?
It's that 'extra something' that makes a star. You have it – or you don't. Since the first show of this name in 2004 about 220,000 young people have tried their luck in the show every year. The X Factor is the biggest TV talent show in Europe. In the UK about 12.7 million people watch the final and choose their favourite.
In the final weeks of the show the ten best sing live. The winner records a single that comes into the shops just before Christmas. It usually becomes the Christmas Number One in the Top Ten charts. That's when a new star is born …

Success – but for how long?
What happens to the winners? Do they really become stars for more than just a year? Do they really start a great career in pop music? And how much money do they really get? One thing is sure: their music managers and bosses get more – much more.

b) What's the article about? Choose A, B or C.

A a TV Top Ten show B a TV music quiz show C a TV talent show for pop singers

c) What's the name of the German TV show that's the same? ____________

4 WORDS Robert's teen magazine (Prepositions) ▸ p. 90

Robert tells Sam about the teen magazine. Complete the text with these prepositions.

about (2x) • after • at (3x) • for • in (4x) • of • to (2x) • with (2x) • without (2x)

Robert Hey, Sam! I must tell you ______ our teen magazine. I'm the editor ______ the music section. I had a video chat ______ my UK friends because they know a lot ______ music and they're good ______ it. Latisha has written about when and where she listens ______ music every day, and ______ the end she writes: 'It would be boring ______ lunchtime ______ school ______ the school radio. ______ school no steel drums – impossible! ______ the evening how would I relax ______ music?' Cool idea, eh?

Sam It's good that you kept ______ touch ______ your British friends. But I'm interested ______ music too.

Robert Well, maybe you could write an article ______ our magazine. It's up ______ you.

5 WRITING COURSE Part 5: A short biography (Correcting your text)

► p. 91, p. 98/P 6 • SF (p. 147)

a) *Your friend's homework was: Write a short biography of a star. He/She wrote about Johnny Depp. Read the text carefully and mark the mistakes in red.*

My star biography: Johnny Depp

Johnny Depp is born on 9 June, 1963, in Kenntucky, USA. When he was seven, moved the family to Florida. He grew up there. He left school when he was 15. He played in different rock bands. He wasn't successfull. He was lucky. He met the actor Nicholas Cage in Los Angeles. That's when his carreer as an actor begun. He worked hardly in small film rolls. He has made his first film in 1984 – *A Nightmare on Elm Street*. For many years he wasn't famous. Depps' big success came in 2003 with his film *Pirates of the Caribbean*. Although he's a big star, he doesn't like Hollywood. He lives in France with french singer Vanessa Paradis and their two children.

Fun fact

When an interviewer asked Johnny Depp's little daughter Lily-Rose, 'What do your parents do?', she answered: 'My mom is a singer and my dad is a pirate.'

6605

b) *There are ten mistakes. Where are they? Write the line number and correct the mistake.*

	Mistake on line:	Correct:
Wrong spelling (2):	3	successful
Missing capital letter:		
Wrong word:		
Wrong tense (2):		
Wrong irregular verb form:		
Wrong word order (SPO):		
Wrong adverb form:		
Wrong possessive form:		

c) **Extra** *How would you improve the text? Tick (✓) the boxes.*

I would …

- use paragraphs. ☐
- use linking words (*and, but, because, so*). ☐
- add a few adverbs (*very, really*). ☐
- add time phrases (*later, soon after that*). ☐

d) *In your exercise book, write the text again with your corrections from b) and your changes in c).*

6 REVISION Weekend plans (Present progressive with future meaning) ▸ p. 92 • GF 7 (p. 155)

What's Robert doing next weekend? Write sentences in the present progressive.

1 Fri: after school – go to the city centre with Sam

On Friday after school he's going to the city centre with Sam.

2 Fri: evening – go to the youth centre

3 Sat: morning – get up early

4 Sat: evening – DJ at a friend's party

5 Sun: after lunch – have another video chat with his friends in the UK

6706

7 WORDS People or things? ▸ p. 92

Put the words into two groups: people and things

recorder • *farmer* • danger • leader • goalkeeper • actor • career • supporter • editor • pepper • sleepover collector • leather • butcher • waiter • cooker • caretaker • monitor

People: *farmer,*

Things: *recorder,*

6707

8 My book quiz ▸ p. 92

How well do you know your student's book?

a) Underline the right answer. The letters after your answers tell you if they are correct.

1 The famous bridge in London that opens for ships is called …

London Bridge. (W)	Tower Bridge. (R)	Westminster Bridge. (C)

2 The names of the main Orkney Islands are Mainland, Flotta and …

Skye. (O)	Kirkwall. (R)	Hoy. (I)

3 L. S. Lowry was a famous …

footballer. (R)	writer. (O)	artist. (G)

4 The London Tube station Queensway is on the …

Circle Line. (G)	Central Line. (H)	Jubilee Line. (S)

5 The capital of Canada is …

Ottawa. (T)	Toronto. (N)	Montréal. (E)

b) On which pages can you find these sentences? Write the page numbers in the boxes.

1 It's a dish that my grandma brought with her from Trinidad. ☐

2 They're just stupid bullies, Katrina. ☐

3 Now we have to find Waterloo and the best way to get there. ☐

4 The bears aren't afraid of us any more. ☐

Now add the page numbers together. If you get 176, your answers are correct.

c) Write answers. Then write a letter from each answer.

1 What's the name of Robert's friend who is having a party on Saturday? Ashley (2) s

2 Which Caribbean island did Mrs Byrd's grandma come from? ________ (3) ___

3 In which town does Katrina go to school? ________ (7) ___

4 What's the name of the place where Asif likes to play video games? (London) ________ (1) ___

5 What's the name of the part of London where Asif lives? (Tower) ________ (1) ___

6 What name did the 'Beauties' call Katrina? ________ (6) ___

7 Which Canadian singer sang the big hit 'Sk8er boi'? ________ (7) ___

▶ *Put the letters in the correct order to write the name of somebody in your book:* ________________.

1 Complete the words.

Robert is going to be the ________r of the music ____t______ of their youth group's teen magazine. You can send an ____t_____, and if it's interesting, they'll ____b________ it. You can
6901 also send photos or d__________. If the magazine is a ___c________, they'll do an e-zine too.

2 Where must you add a reflexive pronoun (myself, etc.) or each other?

Can you imagine __________ a day without music? Music helps you to relax __________.

It makes you feel __________ good. Teenagers usually love music, and they often teach __________ to play an instrument.

Robert taught __________ to DJ. Katrina would like to play the steel drum, and Latisha would like to
6902 play the fiddle. If Katrina lived in Manchester, or if Latisha lived on Hoy, they could teach __________.

3 What are they doing next Saturday night?

1 Robert __________ at the community centre.
6903 *2* Katrina and her dad ______________________________ at a ceilidh.

4 Fill in the missing word.

1 Robert is sure that the youth group's teen magazine will be ______________.

2 For a video chat you need a webcam, a microphone , a monitor and ______________.

3 The American word for 'holiday' is ______________.

4 *Robert:* Did you know the answer to Katrina's ______________?

5 *Sam:* Of course I did. It's the Scottish national instrument – the ______________.

6904 *6* When you write the story of somebody's life, it's called a '______________'.

20 points

Now you

If you were the editor of a teen magazine, what kind of sections, articles, photos and stories would you put in? Say why. Write a long paragraph in your exercise book.

6905
6906 *If I was the editor of a teen magazine, I would ...*

- Hier kannst du deine Antworten im Checkpoint überprüfen. Falls du Probleme mit den jeweiligen Aufgaben hattest, folge den Lernhilfen in der rechten Spalte. Die Verweise beziehen sich auf dein Schülerbuch.
- Deine Punktzahl kannst du ermitteln, indem du dir für jede richtige Lösung einen Punkt gibst. Schreib deine Gesamtpunktzahl in das gelbe Kästchen unten links.

1 Transport: What is it?

1 a ferry
2 a tram
3 a platform
4 a ticket machine
5 a bus stop
6 an airport

6 P.

- Schau dir im Skills File in deinem Buch den Punkt zu *Learning words* (S. 135) an.
- Lern die Wörter mithilfe des Vocabulary (S. 162 und *Word field: Transport*, S. 163) und der Übung 2 im Practice-Teil deines Buchs (S. 20).

2 Have you ever ...?

Asif Have you ever eaten
Robert ate
Have you ever tried
Robert 've eaten
Asif did you have
Robert had

6 P.

- Lies dir Grammar File 1 zum *present perfect* und *simple past* durch (S. 149).
- Löse die Aufgaben 4 (S. 21), 8 (S. 23), 11 und 12a (S. 24) im Practice-Teil.

3 Find and write food words.

1 beef
2 eggs
3 lamb
4 mushrooms
5 onions
6 peas
7 pork
8 vegetables

8 P.

- Lern die Wörter mithilfe des Vocabulary (S. 163 und *Word field: Food*, S. 164).
- Sieh dir die Übung 10a im Practice-Teil (S. 24) noch einmal an.

Now you (Ideas)

take a bus tour/see sights/walk through Hyde Park/ see Buckingham Palace/take photos/buy sandwiches for lunch/great weather/ask the way/take the Tube/ visit Tower of London/see Gherkin and St Paul's/eat at a Bangladeshi restaurant/next day/go on the Eye/ fantastic views of London/see Houses of Parliament/very tired/go to bed early/like best

- Um Ideen über London zu sammeln, kannst du dir die Unit 1 in deinem Buch noch einmal anschauen oder auch im Internet recherchieren.
- Schau im Skills File (S. 146) nach, wie du deine Ideen sammeln und ordnen und deine Sätze interessanter gestalten kannst.
- Die Übung 6 im Practice-Teil (S. 22) zeigt dir noch einmal, wie du deinen Schreibstil verbessern kannst.

Ich habe ______ Punkte von 20.

20–18	Sehr gut. Weiter so!
17–14	Schon recht gut.
Unter 14	Genauer lernen!

1 Town and country: Label the pictures.

6 P.

1 coast
2 rocks
3 cliff
4 bay
5 car park
6 salmon

Falls du Probleme hattest:

- Wie du Wörter besser lernen kannst und worauf du achten musst, erfährst du im Skills File auf der S. 135.
- Diese Wörter findest du im Vocabulary auf den S. 166 und 168 (*Word field: Town and country*).
- Schau dir auch die Aufgabe 1 im Practice-Teil (S. 38) noch einmal an.

2 If I had more pocket money, ...

8 P.

Leo had
Marie would spend
Leo got would save
Marie wanted would find
Leo worked would have to

- Im Grammar File 3 (S. 151) erfährst du, wie du Bedingungssätze (Typ 2) bildest.
- Wiederhole die Aufgaben 10, 11a und 12a im Practice-Teil (S. 42).

3 Computers and mobiles

6 P.

Leo likes to chat to his friends on his computer after school. It's cheaper than phone calls.

He likes to surf the internet too. It's more fun than homework.

Marie likes to send text messages to her friends on her mobile. She thinks it's more fun than instant messages on the computer.

She has a cool logo on her mobile, a picture of her cat, Tabby. And guess what her ringtone is – Tabby too!

- Informationen über elektronische Medien bekommst du auf den S. 33 und 166–167 in deinem Buch.

Now you (Ideas)

go to Kirkwall/see Katrina's school/walk along the coast to see the Old Man of Hoy/take photos/see the oil rigs/go to a ceilidh/take a bus tour of Edinburgh/see the sights/visit Edinburgh Castle/go shopping in Princes Street/eat Scottish shortbread/try haggis/listen to the bagpipes/take photos of Loch Ness/look for Nessie/buy a book about Loch Ness and the Monster/stay the night at a Scottish castle

- Schau dir die Unit 2 in deinem Buch noch einmal an, um Informationen über Schottland zu sammeln.
- Wie du deinen Text gut strukturieren kannst, zeigt dir die Übung 6 im Practice-Teil (S. 40).
- Im Skills File (S. 146) erfährst du mehr zum Thema *using paragraphs*.

Ich habe ______ Punkte von 20.

20–18	Sehr gut. Weiter so!
17–14	Schon recht gut.
Unter 14	Genauer lernen!

1 Label the pictures.

1 goalkeeper
2 running track
3 coach
4 table tennis bat
5 court
6 sledge

6 P.

Falls du Probleme hattest:

- Schau dir im Skills File den Punkt zu *Learning words* (S. 135) noch einmal an.
- Lern die Wörter mithilfe des Vocabulary (S. 171, 174 und *Word field: Sports*, S. 172–173).
- Löse die Aufgabe 2 im Practice-Teil (S. 60).

2 Complete with who, that or where.

1 Nick is the boy who scored two goals in the schools' cup final.

2 A court is a place where you play tennis or badminton.

3 Hockey is a game that you play in a team.

4 Philipp is the exchange student who is staying with the Byrds.

4 P.

- Im Grammar File 4 (S. 152) kannst du nachlesen, wie du Relativsätze bildest.
- Wiederhole die Aufgaben 4–6 im Practice-Teil (S. 61–62).

3 Paraphrasing

1 Fußballstadion:
It's a place where fans can watch football matches.

2 Torwart:
It's the player who stops the ball in the goal.

3 Pokal:
It's a cup that a person or a team gets if they win the final.

3 P.

- Im Skills File (S. 144) erfährst du, wie du am besten beim *paraphrasing* vorgehst.
- Lies dir auch das Grammar File 4 (S. 152) zu den Relativsätzen noch einmal durch.
- Schau dir die Übung 8 im Practice-Teil (S. 63) an und umschreibe die Wörter in den grünen Kästen.

4 Words

Rosehill beat St. Joseph's in the schools' football cup final in Bridgeford last Saturday. At half-time the score was 0–1. Both teams played better after the break, so Nick Scott was really happy when he scored his second goal in the eighty-ninth minute.

7 P.

- Sieh dir die S. 54 und 170–173 in deinem Buch noch einmal an, um die 'Sport'-Wörter zu wiederholen.

Now you (Ideas)

football/fast, exciting, good team sport/can play it at school or in a park/not expensive, can watch it on TV/can be a fan of a football club/can play it against other schools/can play with one or more friends/can read about lots of famous stars/golf/boring, expensive, slow/better for older people than for young people/not a team sport/can't play it at school

- Suche in Unit 3 oder im Internet nach interessanten Informationen über das Thema Sport/Sportarten und bring deine eigene Meinung ein.
- Schau dir im Skills File die S. 146 an, um deinen Text besser strukturieren zu können.

Ich habe ______ Punkte von 20.

20–18	Sehr gut. Weiter so!
17–14	Schon recht gut.
Unter 14	Genauer lernen!

Falls du Probleme hattest:

1 Name the activities.

1 canoeing
2 hunting
3 camping
4 fishing
5 snowshoeing

5 P.

- Lies dir im Skills File die S. 135 noch einmal durch.
- Lern die Wörter mithilfe der S. 69 und 174–175 in deinem Buch.

2 Complete with:

1 won't be able to
2 will have to
3 will be allowed to

3 P.

- Wie du Ersatzverben für modale Hilfsverben verwendest, zeigt dir das Grammar File 6 (S. 154).
- Üben kannst du sie, indem du die Aufgaben 4a und 5 im Practice-Teil (S. 77) noch einmal löst.

3 Complete with until/till, to or by.

1 until/till
2 by
3 to

3 P.

- Schau dir im Vocabulary den blauen Kasten zum *German 'bis'* an (S. 175).

4 Underline the correct part in the bracket.

1 (each other/themselves)
2 (him/himself/ –)
3 (each other/ourselves)
4 (– /herself)

4 P.

- Wie du *reflexive pronouns* und *each other* verwendest, kannst du in den Grammar Files 8 und 9 (S. 155–156) nachlesen.
- Schau dir dazu auch im Vocabulary die blauen Kästen auf den S. 176 und 177 an (*Reflexive pronouns* und *Reflexiv im Deutschen – nicht reflexiv im Englischen*).
- Wiederhole die Übungen 8–10 im Practice-Teil (S. 79).

5 Complete the words.

e asy-going
a nnoying | s trict
g rounded | c omplains

5 P.

- Diese Wörter kannst du dir auf den S. 70 und 175 in deinem Buch anschauen und lernen.
- Löse die Aufgabe 3 im Practice-Teil (S. 76).

Now you (Ideas)

population/geography/what Canadian teenagers like to do in their free time/the bear hunt/famous Canadian singers/Canadian sports and outdoor activities/French in Canada/First Nations people/multi-cultural Canada/immigration

- Durchsuche die Unit 4 nach interessanten Dingen über Kanada.
- Schau dir im Practice-Teil die Übung 7 (S. 78) noch einmal an, um zu erfahren, wie man einen interessanten Text schreiben kann.
- Auch das Skills File (S. 146) kann dir behilflich sein.

Ich habe ______ Punkte von 20.

20–18	Sehr gut. Weiter so!
17–14	Schon recht gut.
Unter 14	Genauer lernen!

1 Complete the words.

Robert is going to be the *editor* of the music *section* of their youth group's teen magazine. You can send an *article*, and if it's interesting, they'll *publish* it. You can also send photos or d*rawings*. If the magazine is a *success*, they'll do an e-zine too.

6 P.

Falls du Probleme hattest:

- Lern die Wörter mithilfe des Vocabulary (S. 178).

2 Where must you add a reflexive pronoun (myself, etc.) or each other?

–	–
–	*themselves*
himself	*each other*

6 P.

- Lies dir die Grammar Files 8 und 9 (S. 155–156) zu den *reflexive pronouns* und *each other* durch.
- Schau dir w im Vocabulary die blauen Kästen auf den S. 176 und 177 an (*Reflexive pronouns* und *Reflexiv im Deutschen – nicht reflexiv im Englischen*).

3 What are they doing next Saturday night?

1 *is DJing*
2 *are playing the fiddle*

2 P.

- Im Grammar File 7 (S. 155) erfährst du mehr zum *present progressive* mit futurischer Bedeutung.
- Wiederhole die Übung 7a im Practice-Teil (S. 99).

4 Fill in the missing word.

1 *successful*
2 *headphones*
3 *vacation*
4 *riddle*
5 *bagpipes*
6 *biography*

6 P.

- Lern die Wörter mithilfe des Vocabulary (S. 178–179).

Now you (Ideas)

articles about famous people/because teenagers who buy teenage magazines like to read about their favourite pop stars, film stars/interesting photos of bands, sports events, stars/interviews with stars/ tips about new films, new books, new computer games/section on fashion/problem pages/interesting web links/useful web addresses/real life stories from readers/letters from readers/quizzes

- Um Ideen zu sammeln, kannst du dir die Unit 5 noch einmal anschauen.
- In der Übung 6 im Practice-Teil (S. 98) erfährst du, wie du deinen Text überprüfen und korrigieren kannst.
- Im Skills File ist auf den S. 146–147 alles zusammengefasst, was du wissen musst, um einen interessanten und gut strukturierten Text zu schreiben.

Ich habe ______ Punkte von 20.

20–18	Sehr gut. Weiter so!
17–14	Schon recht gut.
Unter 14	Genauer lernen!

Unit 1

GF 1 The present perfect and the simple past in contrast ▸ *GF (p. 149)*

a) REVISION The simple past

Last weekend Robert **went** to London with his parents.

In the afternoon they **visited** the Tower, and then they **took** the Tube to Waterloo.

Asif **met** them at the London Eye and they all **had** a great time.

Mit dem ***simple past*** berichtest du über Vergangenes – z. B., wenn du eine Geschichte erzählst.
Das *simple past* drückt aus, dass etwas zu einem **bestimmten Zeitpunkt** oder **in einem bestimmten abgeschlossenen Zeitraum** in der Vergangenheit geschah. (Frage: **Wann?**)
Daher findest du in *simple past*-Sätzen oft **genaue Zeitangaben** wie *last weekend, yesterday, a week ago, in 2005.*

b) REVISION The present perfect

Asif **has** already **visited** the London Trocadero.
... hat schon mal ... besucht

He **has** always **wanted** to go on the London Eye, but he **hasn't done** that yet.
... hat schon immer ... gehen wollen
... hat ... noch nicht getan

He and his friends **have** often **been** to Brick Lane Market.
... sind schon oft ... gewesen

Mit dem ***present perfect*** drückst du aus, dass etwas **irgendwann in der Vergangenheit** geschehen ist.
Daher findest du oft **Adverbien der unbestimmten Zeit** in *present perfect*-Sätzen, z. B.

already	schon (mal)	*always*	(schon) immer
just	gerade (eben)	*never*	(noch) nie
not ... yet	noch nicht	*often*	(schon) oft
ever?	jemals?	*yet?*	schon?

! Beim ***present perfect*** ist der genaue Zeitpunkt des Geschehens nicht wichtig oder nicht bekannt.

c) Present perfect or simple past?

◂ 1 Asif fragt, ob Robert **überhaupt schon mal** türkisch gegessen hat – also ***present perfect***:
Have *you ever* ***tried*** *Turkish food?*

◂ 2 Dann möchte er wissen, **wann** das war, und er fragt daher im ***simple past***:
And when ***did*** *you* ***try*** *it?*

◂ 3 Robert antwortet im ***simple past***, weil er den **genauen Zeitpunkt** nennt:
We ***went*** *to a Turkish restaurant last Saturday.*

Unit 2

GF 2 The *will*-future for spontaneous decisions ▸ *GF (p. 150)*

a) REVISION The *will*-future

Katrina's mum **(Vorhersage)**	Hurry up, Katrina! We**'ll be** late for the ferry.
Katrina **(Vermutung)**	No, we **won't**. I'm ready now. And I think the ferry **will be** a few minutes late anyway.

Mit *will* + Infinitiv kannst du über die Zukunft sprechen. Du verwendest es für Vorhersagen und Vermutungen.

Die Kurzform von *will not* heißt *won't*.

b) Spontaneous decisions

Die Taschen aus der Zeitschrift.
Ich zeig sie dir ... hier, schau.

Du verwendest das *will-future* auch, wenn du einen spontanen (nicht geplanten) Entschluss fasst.
Oft handelt es sich dabei um Hilfsangebote oder Versprechen.

! Im Deutschen steht bei einem spontanen Entschluss meist die Gegenwart. Im Englischen muss das *will-future* stehen:
I'll show you ...
Ich zeig sie dir ...

GF 3 Conditional sentences ▸ *GF (p. 151)*

a) REVISION Conditional sentences (type 1)

Alison If they **choose** you, you'**ll be** a star.
Wenn sie dich wählen, bist du ... /
Wenn sie dich wählen, wirst du ... sein.

Linda If **I don't get** to the shop soon, they **won't have** those trendy new bags any more.

Du kennst bereits Bedingungssätze vom Typ 1 („**Was ist, wenn ...**"-**Sätze**).
Sie sagen aus, was unter bestimmten Bedingungen geschieht oder nicht geschieht:

***if*-Satz (Bedingung)**	**Hauptsatz (Folge)**
*If they **choose** you,*	*you'**ll be** a star.*
simple present	***will-future***

b) Conditional sentences (type 2)

Wenn ein Filmemacher mich für einen seiner Filme auswählen würde, wäre ich berühmt / würde ich berühmt.

Ich würde nicht hier wohnen, wenn ich reich und berühmt wäre.

If I **had** enough money, I could **buy** a new bike.
Wenn ich genug Geld hätte, könnte ich mir ein neues Rad kaufen.

Bedingungssätze vom Typ 2 sind
„**Was wäre, wenn ...**"-**Sätze**.
Sie drücken aus, was unter bestimmten Bedingungen **sein würde**, aber doch eher unwahrscheinlich ist (oder sogar unmöglich):

Es ist unwahrscheinlich, dass Fiona von einem Filmemacher ausgewählt werden wird. Also wird sie wahrscheinlich auch nicht berühmt.

***if*-Satz (Bedingung)**	**Hauptsatz (Folge)**
*If a film-maker **chose** me,*	*I **would be** famous.*
simple past	***would + infinitive***

(Kurzform von *I/you/he/... would: I'd / you'd / he'd / ...*)

! Im *if*-Satz steht **kein *would***. Also nicht:
If a film-maker ~~would choose~~ me, ...

Im Hauptsatz kann auch *could* („könnte") stehen.

Unit 3

GF 4 Relative clauses ▸ *GF (p. 152)*

The girl who plays for United U14s is Latisha.
Das Mädchen, das für die U14 von *United* spielt, ...

Philipp is **an exchange student** who is staying with Latisha.
... ein Austauschschüler, der bei Latisha wohnt.

Mit Relativsätzen sagst du genauer,wen oder was du meinst.

◂ In Relativsätzen, die **Personen** beschreiben, verwendest du ***who***:
the man / the woman / people** who **...
der Mann, der ... / die Frau, die ... / Leute, die ...

There's still **some Maths** that she has to do.
... etwas Mathematik, die sie noch machen muss.

Mrs Byrd has cooked **a dish** that Philipp likes.
... ein Gericht, das Philipp mag.

◂ In Relativsätzen, die **Dinge** (und Tiere) beschreiben, verwendest du ***that***:
the dish / an animal *that* ***...***
das Gericht, das ... / ein Tier, das ...

... **a dish** which Philipp likes
The girl that plays for United U14s ...

Für Dinge (und Tiere) wird auch *which* verwendet.
Und manchmal findest du auch *that* für Personen.

he girl **who plays** football ...
Das Mädchen, **das** Fußball **spielt** ...

! Beachte die unterschiedliche Wortstellung in englischen und deutschen Relativsätzen.

GF 5 Contact clauses ▸ *GF (p. 153)*

Das Relativpronomen kann **Subjekt** oder **Objekt** sein.

1 An artist is somebody **who** paints pictures.
..., **der** Bilder malt.

1 Das Relativpronomen ist **Subjekt des Relativsatzes** (es steht <u>direkt vor dem Verb</u>):

	Subjekt	
An artist is somebody	***who***	*paints pictures.*
Ein Künstler ist jemand,	***der***	*Bilder malt.*
The Lowry is a museum	***that***	*has something for everybody.*
Das Lowry ist ein Museum,	***das***	*für jeden etwas hat.*

2 Beckham is the only player who Philipp knows.
..., den Philipp kennt.

2 Das Relativpronomen ist Objekt **des Relativsatzes**:

	Objekt	Subjekt	
Beckham is the only player	*who*	*Philipp*	*knows.*
Beckham ist der einzige Spieler,	*den*	*Philipp*	*kennt.*
Football is a sport	*that*	*Latisha*	*loves.*
Fußball ist ein Sport,	*den*	*Latisha*	*liebt.*

I don't like football much. David Beckham is the only **player I know**.

Football is a **sport I love**. The **stadium you see** over there is Old Trafford.

An artist is somebody who paints pictures.
(*not:* An artist is ~~somebody paints pictures~~.)

◂ Wenn *who* oder *that* **Objekt** des Relativsatzes ist, wird es manchmal **weggelassen** – wie in den Beispielen links. Relativsätze ohne Relativpronomen nennt man *contact clauses*.

! Achtung:
Wenn das **Relativpronomen direkt vor dem Verb** steht, ist es Subjekt – dann darfst du es **<u>nicht</u> weglassen**!

The **boy Latisha is chatting** with is Banglaboy.
Der Junge, mit dem Latisha chattet, ist Banglaboy.

The **stadium they are looking** at is Old Trafford.

! Beachte die Stellung der Präposition in Relativsätzen mit Verben wie *talk to, chat with, look at, stay with*.
Die Präposition steht an derselben Stelle wie im Hauptsatz:
Latisha is *chatting with* ***Banglaboy.***
The boy ***Latisha is*** *chatting with* ***is Banglaboy.***

Unit 4

GF 6 Modals and their substitutes ▸ GF (p. 154)

a) „können": *can – (to) be able to*

Wenn du sagen willst, dass jemand etwas tun **kann, darf** oder **muss**, dann verwendest du ***can, may, must*** oder ihre **Ersatzverben**:

Katrina can play the fiddle.
Robert doesn't play an instrument, but he's able to DJ. — kann auflegen

– **Gegenwart** (wenn jemand etwas tun **kann**): *can* und *am/is/are able to*

Robert was ill last Saturday, so he wasn't able to DJ. — konnte nicht auflegen

– **Vergangenheit** (wenn jemand etwas tun **konnte**): *was/were able to*

Do you think he'll be able to DJ at Ashley's party? — wird auflegen können

– **Zukunft** (wenn jemand etwas tun **können wird**): *will be able to*

I could **hear** music, but I couldn't **see** anybody.
Ich konnte Musik hören, aber ich konnte niemanden sehen.

Zu *can* gibt es auch die Vergangenheitsform *could*. Sie steht vor allem in verneinten Sätzen und Fragen und mit Verben der Wahrnehmung *(see, hear, …)*.

b) „dürfen": *can, may – (to) be allowed to*

Can/May I go to Ashley's party, Mum?
Are you allowed to go to Ashley's party on Saturday? — Darfst du … gehen?

– **Gegenwart** (wenn jemand etwas tun **darf**): *can, may* und *am/is/are allowed to*

Emily wasn't allowed to go to the youth centre last month. — durfte nicht gehen

– **Vergangenheit** (wenn jemand etwas tun **durfte**): *was/were allowed to*

But she'll be allowed to go to Ashley's party on Saturday. — wird gehen dürfen

– **Zukunft** (wenn jemand etwas tun **dürfen wird**): *will be allowed to*

c) „müssen": *must – (to) have to*

'OK, you can go. But you must be back by ten.'
Emily can go to the party, but she has to be back by ten. — muss zurück sein

– **Gegenwart** (wenn jemand etwas tun **muss**): *must* und *has/have to*

Emily was allowed to go to the party, but she had to be back by ten. — musste zurück sein

– **Vergangenheit** (wenn jemand etwas tun **musste**): *had to*

Emily will have to stay at home tomorrow evening. — wird bleiben müssen

– **Zukunft** (wenn jemand etwas tun **müssen wird**): *will have to*

GF 7 The present progressive with future meaning ▸ GF (p. 155)

I can't come to the phone. I'**m washing** my hair. — … Ich wasche mir gerade die Haare.

Das *present progressive* verwendest du, wenn jemand gerade dabei ist, etwas zu tun.

Robert **is doing** a gig on Friday, and he and his parents **are driving** to their cabin on Saturday morning.

So Robert **isn't going** to Ashley's party at the weekend.

Robert hat am Freitag einen Auftritt, und er und seine Eltern fahren am Samstagmorgen zu ihrer Hütte.

Daher wird Robert am Wochenende nicht zu Ashleys Party gehen.

Du kannst mit dem *present progressive* auch über **feste Pläne** und **Verabredungen** sprechen.

Dabei muss klar sein, dass es sich um etwas Zukünftiges handelt, z.B. durch eine Zeitangabe wie *on Friday, next week, at the weekend, tomorrow*.

GF 8 Reflexive pronouns ▸ *GF (pp. 155–156)*

Reflexivpronomen *(ourselves, itself, yourself, ...)* bezeichnen dieselbe Person oder Sache wie das Subjekt *(we, a bear, you, ...)*:

Subjekt		Reflexivpronomen	
We	*have to protect*	*ourselves*	*from the bears.*
A bear	*just wants to feed*	*itself*	*and its babies.*

Wir müssen uns vor den Bären schützen.
Ein Bär will nur sich und seine Babys ernähren.

Reflexive pronouns

Singular		Plural	
myself	(ich) mir/mich	**ourselves**	(wir) uns
yourself	(du) dir/dich	**yourselves**	(ihr) euch
himself	(er) sich	**themselves**	(sie) sich
herself	(sie) sich		
itself	(er/sie/es) sich		

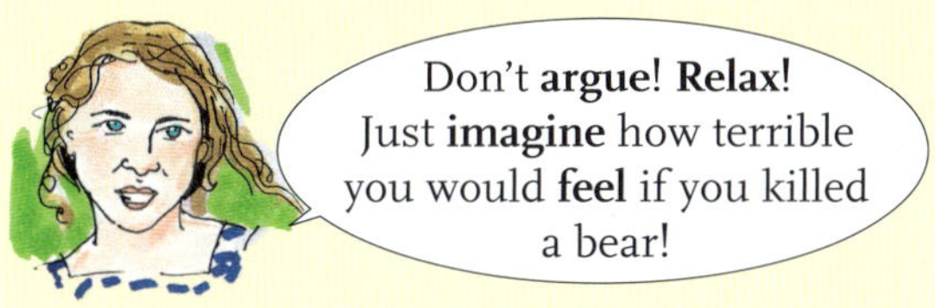

Einige Verben, die im Deutschen mit „sich" gebraucht werden, stehen im Englischen ohne Reflexivpronomen.

Beispiele:	*(to) argue*	sich streiten
	(to) feel	sich fühlen
	(to) imagine sth.	sich etwas vorstellen
	(to) relax	sich entspannen

(Weitere Beispiele ▸ *Vocabulary*, S. 177)

GF 9 Reflexive pronoun or *each other*? ▸ *GF (p. 156)*

Robert and Asif are taking photos of themselves.
Robert und Asif machen Fotos von sich (selbst).

Für **„sich"** im Sinne von **„sich selbst"** benutzt du die Pronomen auf ***-self/-selves***:
I – myself, he – himself, they – themselves usw.

◂ Robert und Asif machen Fotos von sich selbst – Robert fotografiert sich selbst, und Asif fotografiert sich selbst.

Now they are taking photos of each other.
Jetzt fotografieren sie sich gegenseitig. /
Jetzt machen sie Fotos voneinander.

Für **„sich"** im Sinne von **„sich gegenseitig"** oder **„einander"** benutzt du ***each other***.

◂ Robert und Asif fotografieren sich gegenseitig – Robert fotografiert Asif, und Asif fotografiert Robert.

(Statt *each other* wird auch *one another* verwendet:
Now they are taking photos of one another.)

Illustrationen

Roland Beier, Berlin (S. 10; S. 13–15; S. 19; S. 22 unten; S. 27; S. 31 oben; S. 32; S. 38; S. 40; S. 47 Bild 1–6, Schiefertafel; S. 49; S. 54 unten Bild 1–6; S. 59 Bild 1–5, Schiefertafel; S. 64; S. 69 oben; S. 75–79); Constanze Schargan, Berlin (S. 16; S. 22 oben Bild 1–6; S. 25; S. 30; S. 31 unten; S. 47 unten; S. 50–54 oben; S. 59 unten; S. 67; S. 69 unten)

Bildquellen

Alamy, Abingdon (S. 5 li.: PhotosIndia.com LLC; S. 7 sandwiches: Cloe Johnson, train: Ashley Cooper; S. 8 Brick Lane: Marion Bull, Trocadero: Andrew Holt; S. 13 Bild 5: Trevor Smithers ARPS; S. 14 Mitte: PhotosIndia.com LLC/Batch 7; S. 16 Bild 5: Peter Forsberg; S. 17 Bild D: Bettina Strenske; S. 24 re.: Doug Houghton; S. 26: JUPITERIMAGES/BananaStock; S. 29 li.: Photodisc/Malcolm Fife; S. 50 Bild 1: david sanger photography, Bild 2: RubberBall/Mike Kemp; S. 55 oben: Design Pics. Inc/Carson Ganci); Britta Bensmann, Berlin (S. 13 Bild 1); John Birdsall Social Issues Photolibrary, Nottingham (S. 1–2; S. 5 re.; S. 6 Bild 2 u. 3; S. 7 Robert; S. 14 li. u. re.; S. 18; S. 28; S. 50 Bild 3); Corbis, Düsseldorf (S. 29 re.: Atlantide Phototravel/Massimo Borchi); Gareth Evans, Berlin (S. 23); Getty Images, München (S. 16 Bild 3: Ian Kckinnell; S. 39 Bild 4: Tim Graham Photo Library; S. 56: Laura Ciapponi); Jennifer Seidl, München (S. 8 Hyde Park; S. 9 oben; S. 17 Bild C u. F; S. 41; S. 43); Picture Alliance, Frankfurt/Main (S. 39 Bild 2: KPA Honorar und Belege; S. 66: dpa-Report/Walt Disney Pictures); Shutterstock, New York (S. 6 Bild 1: Stuart Miles, Bild 4: Tracy Whiteside; S. 7 violin case (M): Laura Frenkel, bags (M): maxstockphoto, train station: Vivek Agrawal; S. 8 London Eye: photogl, Tower of London: Lance Bellers; S. 9 unten re.: Axel Wolf; S. 10: Bryan Busovicki; S. 12 (u. 13 Bild 1 postcard): Bartlomiej K. Kwieciszewski; S. 13 Bild 2: Paduraru Catalin Alexandru, Bild 3: Olga&Elnur, Bild 4: Louis Michaud, Bild 6 shirts: Graca Victoria, jeans: pixelman, Bild 7: Elnur, Bild 8: Timothy Large; S. 16 Bild 1: Sheffield Wakefield, Bild 2: martin garnham, Bild 4: Andy Lindon; S. 17 Bild A: Jarno Gonzalez Zarraonandia, Bild B: Chris Jenner, Bild E: Christopher Dodge, Bild G: Simone van den Berg; S. 24 li.: David Woods; S. 31 Bild 1: Marco Regalia, Bild 2: Galina Barskaya, Bild 3: Stephen Bonk, Bild 4: Peter Clark, Bild 5: vladimir maravic, Bild 6: Tischenko Irina; S. 39 Bild 1: Amy Nicole Harris, Bild 3: Jo Chambers, Bild 5: David Woods; S. 42 (u. 60) British flag: Chris Harvey, German flag: Kurt De Bruyn; S. 44 oben: Anthony Monterotti, unten: Magdalena Bujak; S. 49: SpeedKingz; S. 55 unten: marianad; S. 58 oben u. unten: nialat; S. 60 unten: Natalia Bratslavsky; S. 65: Zoom Team); Transport for London, London (S. 9 unten li.)

Titelbild

Alamy, Abingdon (London Eye (M): Ian MacPherson); Corbis, Düsseldorf (bus (M): Royalty-Free); IFA-Bilderteam, Ottobrunn (Union Jack: Jon Arnold Images)